"In *Reach Your Summit and Beyond*, Deb Roffe shares her love of the mountains and climbing to give the reader a fabulous perspective of how we can reach our goals and dreams while enjoying the journey along the way. She used a delightful combination of coaching and personal stories to deliver a worthy message."

Lisa Shultz, co-author of *Speaking Your Truth* and *How To Bring Your Book To Life This Year* www.LisaShultz.com

"A book begins with a person. Deb Roffe is an exceptional human being. She has made a significant impact on my life as my friend and coach. Give yourself the gift of Deb in your life...Read this book, study it, and LIVE IT! I promise it will change your life!"

Michael Charest, Author, *From Grunt to Greatness,* President, Business Growth Solutions www.BGSllc.com

"*Reach Your Summit and Beyond* is truly a step-by-step guide that will help you actualize your dreams. Take this book and treasure it every step of the way, it's a book you'll want to come back to again and again!"

Andrea Costantine, author of *Soulful Marketing: Heart Centered Marketing for Conscious Entrepreneurs*

"*Reach Your Summit and Beyond* is a powerful, inspirational and practical guide for living your dreams. It is a must read for anyone wanting to create positive change in their lives."

Karen Mehringer, author of *Sail Into Your Dreams: 8 Steps to Living a More Purposeful Life*

"You deserve to live the life of your dreams and Deb's book, Reaching Your Summit and Beyond, will inspire you to do it! Give yourself the gift of this book and Deb will step by step teach you how to overcome your saboteur and reach your own personal summit. An amazing life coach, Deb will enable you to: Face your fears. Climb over the "boulders" in your life. Feel invigorated and empowered. Take your DREAMS to REALITY!"

Karin Krueger

"In *Reaching Your Summit And Beyond*, Deb Roffe demonstrates that she's lived the peaks and valleys of life to reach her summit. With authenticity and honest self-disclosure, Deb becomes our loving and encouraging companion on our own climb to our peak and beyond. Whether this is our first attempt or our 20th, her wisdom— along with her gentle and direct guidance—provide the compass and the roadmap to move us toward the top of the mountain to live the life of our dreams!"

Donna Mazzitelli, Bellisima Living, LLC

"As someone exploring new career avenues, I took everything Deb Roffe talks about in *Reach Your Summit and Beyond* to heart. Besides offering good practical strategies, she provides inspiration—perhaps the most important ingredient of all in making a life change. Reading this book helped me remember to persevere as well as not let my dream fall by the wayside."

Daryn Eller

"Deb has transformed her years of hiking and love of the mountains into a metaphor for our life journeys. Let her experiences in this book lead you to the growth and transformation you'd love to see in your own life."

Christy Strauch, author of *Your Marketing Personality, and Passion, Plan, Profit: 12 Simple Steps to Convert Your Passion into a Solid Business.*

# REACH YOUR SUMMIT AND BEYOND

## A Step-by-Step Guide to Achieving Your Personal Peak

Deb Roffe
*With Stefanie Rittner*

Book Title: Reach Your Summit and Beyond: A Step-by-Step Guide to Achieving Your Personal Peak

Copyright © 2011 Deb Roffe

Printed in the United States of America

Cover design: Bekka Sciarro
Editing: Daryn Eller
Illustrations: Bekka Sciarro
Book layout and design: Andrea Costantine
Author photograph: Teri Virbickis

ISBN 978-1-46107-381-9
First Edition

For Mom, Betty Dohn,
the one who was always there, who encouraged us, drove
us, and waved us off each time; the one who stood at the
beginning and end of every trail.


For Dad, Donald Dohn,
the one who kindled the dream,
inspired us to reach the summit,
and taught us the true meaning of the mountains.

Mount of the Holy Cross, 1971,
Scott Pratt, David Dohn, Doug Dohn, Dad, and Deb

# Acknowledgements

Stefanie, without you, this book would still be an idea left out on the hiking trails. You grabbed my dream and truly made it a reality. All of the climbing, sweat, and tears that went into summiting those 14ers made this vision evolve. It's hard to believe this idea began on a trail one day as a distant dream. I am forever grateful for all of your hard work, dedication, and commitment to getting this book done. You kept it going, even when I had doubt.

To my husband Kirby, you are my mountain. Your endless support is the reason I am here today. You saw the dream on the trails with me, and have encouraged me along the way. I can't thank you enough for being my personal cheerleader all of these years. Without you, I know I would have never reached my own personal peak.

My children, Greg, Michael, and Matt, and daughter-in-law Tabitha: Thank you for standing behind me every step of the way through all of my adventures. Your belief in me has kept me going, even when I have wanted to turn back.

To the supportive people who helped this book come to life in all of the little bits and pieces, Andrea Costantine for being there at the beginning and seeing this through at the end, to Daryn Eller for your excellence, ideas, and dedication, and to Bekka Sciarro for your creativity and illustrations. Lastly, to Donna Mazzitelli for your keen eye.

# Table of Contents

# ∿ *Foreword* ∿

When I first met Deb, I never imagined that our relationship would become what it is now. Mothers-in-law are known to be difficult, controlling, and invasive. Marrying into a family with faults and flaws (much like my own family) was bound to be challenging. But despite those characteristics, all the members of this family shared one special quality: they loved the mountains. And so did I—I just didn't know it yet.

It was the summer of 2005. We had finally decided to go. Greg and I had talked about hiking a Colorado 14er with his family for several years but never followed through on the idea. Sure, I liked hiking, but 14,000 feet was no small task. That year Greg's grandpa was turning 80 and he wanted to climb Mount of the Holy Cross one more time. We decided that if an eighty-year-old could do it, surely so could we.

The day I summitted my first 14er was life changing. Standing 14,005 feet high on Holy Cross was literally breathtaking. I remember laughing and crying at the same time, knowing that I wanted more. More mountains, more challenges, and more for my life. While standing on what felt like the top of the world, I was mesmerized by the view, with being on top, and with my victory. Even so, I wouldn't realize until a few years later what that day actually meant to me. The greatest lesson I learned wasn't from reaching the summit; it was in the journey. After that first summit, my relationship with my in-laws began to change drastically. For the next several years through miles and miles of forest trails, their appreciation and understanding of nature rubbed off on me. I fell in love with Deb and her family and I fell in love with hiking. Deb had always talked about the mountain as a metaphor for life. She explained to me that, "If you can climb a 14er, you can do anything in life." I was skeptical at first, but I have watched Deb live out this statement over the past several years. I have seen her ideas become dreams and her dreams become reality. She has encouraged me to reach higher, to go farther, and to dream big.

From my journey through and up some of Colorado's most beautiful mountains, I have gained the creativity, the hope, and the strength to make my dreams come true. When I am in the presence of my Creator and enjoying all He has made here on earth for me to see, I become inspired. Ever since I was a little girl I have wanted to become a writer and illustrator. During each hike up my some nineteen 14ers, I have imagined being able to write and share these stories with others. This book, which I helped Deb compose, is my first published piece of writing and literally a dream come true.

I am grateful to have worked on this project with Deb and to now be able to share it with each of you.

I have enjoyed the lessons Deb has taught me from the mountains and the ones we have learned together. I am blessed to be a part of her family and to be part of "the dream" Deb envisioned long ago. It is our pleasure to share these gifts and lessons from the mountains with each of you. My hope is that you will be motivated, inspired, and ready to "do" : do more, do the unthinkable, and do whatever it is that you love to do.

Your friend and fellow dreamer,
*Stefanie Rittner*
(Deb's little Mountain Goat)

> *"Today is your day! Your mountain is*
> *waiting so.... get on your way!"*
> \- Dr. Seuss

Stef, Deb, and Delilah at Horsetooth, Fort Collins, CO

# When You're Up
# in the Woods

*"When you're up in the woods where the pine
trees grow, let the sunshine smile on you..."*
- "The Pines," family song by Fred Pratt

# ≈ *Introduction* ≈

Love and appreciation for the mountains has been passed down from generation to generation in my family. I always say it's in our blood. Being part of the Dohn family requires strength, determination, and a love of the outdoors. We even have a family song about the great outdoors, written by my Great Grandpa Pratt in the 1800's. This song has carried us over miles and miles of mountain trails. As a family, we have always been attracted to the mountains, drawn by their splendor and brilliance.

Every summer when my father was a kid, his mother would drive the family from Buffalo, New York, to the woods of Allegheny State Park. They'd camp for months at a time. This was in the 1920's and 30's when specialized camping equipment was not available. They'd set up their simple tents, cook over open fires, swim in the creeks, and just enjoy being in nature. Not surprisingly, my father carried on the tradition when he had his own family, introducing my brothers and me to the joys of camping.

I grew up in Shaker Heights, Ohio, where my family was known for being adventurous, daring, and risk-taking. We frequently went backcountry skiing, drove across the country, and camped out for weeks at a time. The sky was the limit. Just as my Grandma Dohn drove my father to the woods, my own mother would load up the station wagon with kids and skiing and camping equipment, then drive over twenty-four hours to Colorado. My father was a renowned neurosurgeon with limited time off, but he would always make the effort to show us the ins and outs of backpacking, camping, and hiking. If he couldn't drive with us to Colorado, he would fly out and meet us on the mountain. We were very unique in this way, and the adventurous spirit of the Dohn family was ingrained in me at an early age. I had an attraction, a strong desire, a longing to be in the mountains. It was in nature that I felt alive, inspired, and ready to create.

My admiration for the mountains and understanding of their majesty grew even deeper during the summer of 1971. Several months after my eighteenth birthday, my family set out to hike to the top of a mountain. As a teenager, I was spirited, strong, and energetic. Being the only girl in the family, I had quickly learned how to keep up with my two brothers. Any type of physical activity they could do, I could do. I was determined, I never complained, and nothing could hold me back, not even a 14,000-foot mountain. After backpacking in the Gore Range outside of Vail, Colorado, for an entire week, we were going to conclude our trip by climbing Mount of the Holy Cross. This wasn't just any old mountain. Not only was the peak 14,005 feet high, but Holy Cross was a legend both in the Rocky Mountains and among members of the Dohn family.

The hiking party included me, my dad, Don, my two brothers, David and Doug, a family friend, and my cousins, the Pratt's. The night before, we hiked over Half Moon Pass and set up a base camp. Even if our equipment was better than my father's family had in the 20's and 30's, this was still only 1971 and our gear was far inferior to the type of equipment available now. We wore jeans, leather boots, thick wool socks, and carried heavy tents in heavy packs with heavy metal frames. The grueling climb over and into the pass took a toll on our bodies, especially because we were "flatlanders" from Ohio.

Tired and sore, we arose early the next morning to start our ascent up Holy Cross. I had heard all about this mountain and the history of the people who made the trek up its peak in the 1800's, following it with a descent down into the Bowl of Tears to dip their prayer cloths into its holy water. My parents had an old leather-bound book about Holy Cross that was filled with black and white pictures of the courageous men and women in suspenders, wool coats, dresses, bonnets, and lace-up leather shoes completing their pilgrimage across the ridge. The pages explained how the mountain received its name when, each year, the snow melted leaving only a swatch of white in a large crevice on the mountain's face, forming a giant cross. It was believed to be a mountain of healing, one with a strong spiritual essence. As I stood before the peak, it was an astounding sight to see. The photographs etched in my memory came to life right before my eyes. I was in awe.

We started up the mountain and quickly got into a rhythm, my dad leading the way. I remember walking behind him, following in his footsteps and taking in the breathtaking view. Even at the young age of eighteen I felt something magical in the spirit of the mountain, although it would take me years to recognize it to the extent that I do now.

The trail switch-backed through the trees and we slowly zigzagged our way along. I welcomed the cool shade and enjoyed the tranquil feeling of being surrounded by the forest. As we hiked, the trees grew sparser until, finally, there weren't any at all. We passed through open fields of alpine tundra filled with tiny grasses and flowers. I was surrounded by beauty. The ground gradually became rockier until there was nothing but large boulders. We had gained a significant amount of altitude and I could see the tips of surrounding peaks.

After climbing through the endless field of boulders, the path marked only by cairns every twenty or so feet, we were nearing the top. The 5,400-foot elevation gain and hours of exertion had left my legs weak and my head dizzy. Rows of mountain peaks began to come into fuller view as we ascended higher and higher. It was as if I could reach out and touch the clouds overhead. I paused for a moment to look over at the range of mountains across the way and breathe in their magnificence. We were so incredibly high!

As we took the final steps towards the summit, I had no idea how life changing this climb would be. When I reached the top, something miraculous happened. For the first time, I realized that I could accomplish whatever I wanted to in life. If I could climb this mountain, I really could do anything! It was in this moment that I discovered something bigger than myself. That something or someone had to exist. The beauty and glory of this place simply could not be present without the work of some divine entity. There were mountains and mountains, as far as my eyes could see. To the east, to the west, the north, and the south … they stood like an audience and they were all applauding my accomplishment. It was an astonishing sight. I literally felt my heart leap as I spun around and took in the view. I spread my arms wide and welcomed the feeling. I was standing on top of the world!

It was then that I began to dream. I dreamt about other mountains I could climb. I dreamt about my future. I dreamt about accomplishing the unthinkable. I didn't know at the time where those dreams would take me, but I was dreaming nonetheless.

Holy Cross was just the first of many 14ers I would conquer in my life. Over the years, I enjoyed many more backpacking trips with my family and friends, but it was that initial trip which taught me anything is possible if you dream big, plan, prepare, and persevere. The mountains are a metaphor for life and you don't have to have the slightest interest in hiking to learn the lessons they offer. You have the power to create the vision of what you really want in life and to achieve it. It's a journey, one that can be rocky at times, but it's a journey well worth taking.

Dreaming about my future as I stood on the summit of the Mount of Holy Cross, I didn't know that my life would ultimately have considerable ups and downs. But I have always been able to come back to that moment when I realized that I could accomplish whatever I wanted to and use it as inspiration to get my life back on track. With that as my guiding principle I've learned that taking certain methodical steps—just as you would if you were going to climb a mountain—can get you where you want to go. It's those steps that I want to share with you in this book.

This book is for anyone who has ever felt stuck in a job or an unhappy relationship. It's for anyone looking to live a healthier, less stressed, and more pleasurable life. If you want to give your life more meaning or to reach life goals that you've let fall by the wayside, this is the book for you, too. Each chapter will introduce you to strategies and tools that will help you understand what aspects of your life need to change and how to go about changing them. The chapters are steps on a continuum, each lesson building upon the previous one. Change, of course, doesn't happen overnight; instead it's a process that takes time. But each step will move you closer to capturing the life you've always dreamt of. Remember, climbing a mountain is no small task, but it is not impossible. My hope is that you will understand that you too can climb (metaphorical) mountains. Whatever it is you have been dreaming of, wanting to change, or wishing to accomplish—you can do it! Start right now. Take the journey with me from the trailhead, through the trees, over the boulder fields, and up to the summit!

*Deb Roffe*

Deb with her dad and brothers singing
the family song.

# *Discovering Your Dream*
## *Getting a Glimpse of the Peak*

*"Go confidently in the direction of your
dreams. Live the life you have imagined."*
- Henry David Thoreau

# ≋ *Chapter One* ≋

After my ascent of Holy Cross, real life stepped in and the amazing dreams I had envisioned on that day in 1971 slowly started to fade. Over the years they became replaced with the demands of children, work, and other commitments. During the course of the next thirty-four years, my love of nature remained, but I rarely had a chance to go backpacking. Life had gotten complicated, messy, and busy. There were too many distractions, I was too out of shape, I didn't have the time ... any excuse worked. The upshot was that life had gotten in the way, and I wasn't climbing mountains any more, real or metaphorical.

By 2005 my extended family had grown to include husbands, wives, children, nieces, nephews, and their girlfriends and boyfriends. My parents had divorced. My mother, my brothers, and I moved out and settled down in Colorado, then us kids had our own families. I had been married, then divorced, then married again, the second time around to Kirby, my high school sweetheart from Shaker Heights. The oldest of my three sons had just become engaged and would be graduating from college soon. I had been a nurse for almost thirty years and I was ready for a change. My dad had retired from neurosurgery, remarried, and was aging. How had life passed by so incredibly fast?

In August of that year, my dad, now known as Grandpa Dohn, was turning eighty. To honor both his wisdom about the outdoors and his eightieth birthday, we all decided to return to the mountain we had often talked about, dreamt about, and shared stories about with our children. We were going to hike Holy Cross again. Dad was going to stand on its peak just one last time.

After months of planning, training, borrowing, and buying equipment, our large family took off on our adventure. The group consisted of my husband, Kirby, my oldest son, Greg, his fiancée, Stefanie, my youngest son, Matt, my dad, and me. We backpacked over Half Moon Pass to our base camp. The next morning some of us were up before daylight to start the ascent of the mountain. There was a lot of excitement, anticipation, and nervousness; no one but Dad and myself had ever climbed a 14er before.

As the hike began, we quickly fell into our line of order, with my dad leading the way as he had always done. He set the perfect pace for the group and as we ventured through the forest we reminisced about old times, recollected memories of family and friends, and told classic Dohn stories. I was thrilled to be back in this place with my father and to take part in such a meaningful journey to the summit with him.

But about two-thirds of the way up, my dad turned to me and said, "Deb, I can't go any farther." I was shocked. I'd never in my life heard my dad speak those words. We all stood in silence while we caught our breath. He was the leader, the pathfinder, the person we leaned on. He was the one who had always given us words of encouragement, such as, "It's just around the corner. Don't give up. Put one foot in front of the other. Let's sing a song." At first I tried to convince him to keep going, to make it to the top this one last time. He said again, "No, Deb. It's okay. I'll be okay. You guys keep going." In that moment I knew what my dad was saying to me. *Now it's your turn Deb. You show the next generation of this family what the mountains mean. You pass on the mountains' gifts, lessons, power, inspiration, and glory.* It was as if he was handing the baton to me. It was my turn to lead. In that instant everything seemed to hold still. It will always be burned into my memory: the steepness of the trail, the beautiful tiny tundra flowers, the beginning of the boulders, and the vastness of the deep blue sky. We all had tears in our eyes as we watched my dad go back down the trail by himself.

After I had caught my breath and wiped away the tears, I knew I had to keep going. I had to be that strong eighteen-year-old again, the girl who was driven and full of dreams. Dad's silhouette disappeared back into the trees, and we all started up the boulder field. It was strange how this mountain, which is one of the more difficult 14ers to climb, was so easy to summit that day. Dad's dream had begun to spread to each one of us. His presence combined with the spiritual energy of the mountain compelled us over the incredible boulder fields, through the snowflakes, and to the summit. It was truly an amazing experience. On the trail, I fell into last place, at the back of the line, so I could push Matt, Greg, and Stefanie the rest of the way. Again the excitement built as we got closer and closer to the top.

Once we were standing on the summit, Greg turned to me and said, "Mom, I have been hearing about this mountain all my life. And I'm finally here." Stef was smiling through teary eyes, taking in the panoramic view. Matt and Kirby were celebrating. And right away I knew their lives would be changed forever. Yes, I thought to myself, the next generation understands; it's in their blood!

31

Feeling the power of the mountain, I looked out and again soaked it all in. It was a bittersweet moment, standing there with my children, but knowing that I would never stand on another peak with my father. It was now my responsibility to carry on the tradition, to keep the mountains a part of our family. This time on Holy Cross I felt different. The dreams I once had here came rushing back to me. This time I was going to make them come true.

When I returned home, I continued dreaming about how my life could be different. I had been doing the same job for the last thirty years. I was a nurse in a gastrointestinal lab, and I performed the same procedures day in and day out. I worked in an enclosed room with no windows, with patients who were unconscious. There were no opportunities for me to interact with anyone, be creative, or grow. My job was mindless, boring, and unfulfilling. I had often wondered what my life would be like had I chosen a different profession. I wished I would have chosen to be a counselor, a therapist, maybe even a teacher—something more rewarding than what I ended up doing. But, I told myself, it was too late, too expensive, and too risky to change my career this late in the game. I had planned on living and dying in that G.I. lab even though the thought of staying much longer was absolutely agonizing.

The day I climbed Holy Cross in honor of my father's 80th birthday, I finally could imagine doing something else. I could now see the possibilities of making a career change, even at 52 years old. After the climb, I started looking into life coach training programs, and that summer I signed up for classes to become a certified life coach. By the following year I had finished my training and created two businesses, Summit Life Coaching and The Nurse Coach. My clientele continued growing and I started doing workshops and retreats. In December 2008, I quit my job as a nurse and started coaching full time. Finally, I was closer to the life I had dreamed of so long ago.

\* \* \*

In life, we often just go through the motions. We get caught up in the daily tasks required by our jobs and families. As a result, our own desires become distant whispers and faded memories. We get comfortable in our lives; I know I got comfortable as a G.I. nurse, even though I was miserable. We tell ourselves it will be too much work, too scary, or even too selfish to make our personal dreams come true. Sometimes we don't even realize we have these dreams or desires in the first place.

It is all too easy to focus on what life expects from you, forgetting what you really expect out of life. Now is the time to discover your dream and find out what you want for your life. Getting a glimpse of what is possible and seeing your full potential is the first step to discovering your dreams. For instance, even before I choose which mountain I am going to climb in Colorado, I see myself reaching the top. In the same way, you must start believing that you can reach your life's "peak." Envision yourself accomplishing your wildest dreams. What would those dreams look like? What could you see yourself doing if you had no constraints holding you back? For a moment put aside your role as a spouse, parent, employee, or boss and allow yourself to dream...

## Discovering the Dream,
## Step 1: What Inspires You?

Take some time to discover what you really want out of life. Here are a few questions to get your ideas flowing.

List all of the things you wanted to be as a child (a teacher, a rock star, an actress):

_____

_____

_____

_____

_____

_____

_____

_____

What are some goals you had when you were younger but haven't yet accomplished?

_____

_____

_____

_____

_____

_____

_____

_____

List at least three things you are very passionate about.

_____

_____

_____

_____
_____
_____

What types of activities make you lose a sense of time?

_____
_____
_____
_____
_____
_____
_____
_____

If you had all the money you needed what would you do with your time?

_____
_____
_____
_____
_____
_____
_____

# Discovering the Dream,
# Step 2: The Wheel of Life

Ginny, a 39-year-old school teacher was at her wits' end. Nothing seemed to be going right, yet she couldn't quite put her finger on what was going on in her life that was causing her unhappiness. She was working full-time, had two children at home, and a husband who traveled frequently for his work. She was stuck doing the majority of the household chores and taking care of the children, which left little time for her to stop and enjoy life. This imbalance all became clearer to Ginny when she completed the "Wheel of Life." Together, we started working on each area one by one, until one day her life gained greater equilibrium. When we redid the wheel six months later, Ginny couldn't believe how much things had improved for her.

The eight sections of this wheel represent different aspects of your life. The outer edge of the wheel is equal to ten and the center, where the lines of the sections meet, is a one. Using a pencil, shade in each section to represent your satisfaction with that part of your life on a scale of one to ten. So, for instance, if you're in the money section and your satisfaction is a three, shade in about one-third of the way up.

Complete this exercise for each section, then look at the new circle you've created. Is it uneven? Where are the imbalances? What areas of your life need improvement? Use this diagram as a roadmap to help you work on the weaker aspects of your life. Revisit it periodically to chart your progress.

## Complete the Wheel of Life

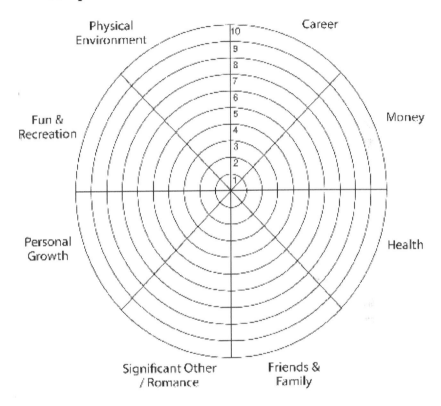

## Discovering the Dream,
## Step 3: Create a Vision Board

One of my clients' favorite workshops is my Vision Board Workshop, which focuses on bringing dreams into reality. Creating a vision board is simple; you can easily do it on your own or you could attend one my workshops and do it within a supportive group. To do it on your own, simply get a poster or piece of tag board. Gather a handful of your favorite magazines and skim through the pages, cutting out any images that speak to you. They could be depictions of material items such as a new house, or a vacation destination, or they could be images that evoke a feeling, such as harmony or peace, that you want to create in your life. The pictures could reflect a new career, a new relationship, or an accomplishment. This is a time for dreaming, not practicality. There does not need to be a reason behind why you like an image; simply cut it out if you find yourself attracted to it. Use pictures, colors, words, and phrases. Once you've finished cutting out the images, arrange them on the poster board in a way that makes the most sense to you. If you have specific dreams or goals already, record them on your board. You may even want to write names, dates, or numbers that go hand-in-hand with your goals. Once your board is completed, hang it in a place where you can see it frequently. (You can always hang it up and continue to add images and words to it later, as you continue dreaming.)

You can also create different vision boards for different dreams and goals in your life. For example, one of my clients created a vision board showing what she wanted her summer to be like. She was ready to enjoy the summer, have fun, and take some time off, so she filled her vision board with images of lounging outside, a picture of her cruiser bike, picnics, and hiking. She created that vision board in March, and in August she wrote me to share how everything on her board came to pass over those summer months.

Be creative when making your vision board. Make one for your career, another for your relationships, one for a dream vacation, or any other goal that you want to see manifest.

"Dreams do come true!" Here's a preview of one of my vision boards when I wanted to quit nursing and start coaching full time.

This week, let your imagination run wild. Revisit old dreams and discover new ones. Whether they're realistic or not, ask yourself "What if?" and see what answers you find. Even if you are not sure where these dreams will lead you, let yourself consider them. There is no need to commit to anything yet; just simply think about the possibilities. Get a glimpse of your "peak."

*"You see things; and you say, 'Why?' But I dream things that never were; and I say, 'Why not?'"*

- George Bernard Shaw

## One Step Closer...

Today you started envisioning more for your life. This is a success in itself! As you dream this week, record your thoughts, inspirations, and feelings. Write down what you hope to accomplish at the end of this journey.

Mount of the Holy Cross, 2005,
Kirby, Matt, Deb, Stef, and Greg

CHAPTER TWO

# *Committing to the Journey*
## *Deciding to Make the Climb*

*"Commitment unlocks the doors of imagination,
allows vision, and gives us the 'right stuff' to
turn our dreams into reality."*
- James Womack

# ᗰ *Chapter Two* ᗰ

Every time I set out to climb a 14er, I make sure that I am entirely committed to the task. Even before I have chosen which mountain to climb and before I set foot near the trailhead, I commit to journeying all the way up to the summit. If I haven't completely decided that I am going to make the climb, then it probably won't happen. I may be interested in hiking a particular mountain, but if I don't fully commit, I may never reach the summit.

We all have dreams and desires, but many of us don't act upon them. **A decision is a commitment to act.** Before you can begin to make your dreams a reality, you have to *decide* that you are going to take action and you must be *committed* to the journey. When you set out to achieve something, whether it is to land a new job or to lose weight, it is normal to want to hurry up and get to the good part. But like anything else, reaching your goals is a process— and sometimes it is a difficult one. This is why most people avoid taking action in the first place. As with climbing a mountain, the journey can be long and arduous, but the end result is always worth it. If you commit to the journey and fully decide to make the climb, you will be successful in reaching your peak.

In 1988, I made one of the most difficult commitments of my life. That was the year I decided to go into treatment and fully commit to recovering from bulimia. I had tried to stop on my own. I had tried counseling. I had even gone into treatment before. But I didn't truly begin my recovery process until I decided to get help for myself rather than because others wanted me to. It was only then that I was able to commit to getting better.

I developed my eating disorder in college. Shortly after moving to Colorado and starting classes at Colorado State University (CSU), I began bingeing and purging. The pressure to succeed in school and be thin as well as being on my own so far away from home was overwhelming. I began restricting foods to stay thin, but then I would end up in a frenzy of binging and purging. It started out as an occasional thing, but quickly became a habit, and then eventually an addiction.

I was the daughter of a renowned neurosurgeon and I was a perfectionist. I put an enormous amount of pressure on myself to do well in school and to make my parents proud. I started worrying that maybe I wasn't smart enough, disciplined enough, pretty enough, or thin enough to accomplish all of my goals. And though I loved living in Colorado, I missed my family and had just broken up with my high school sweetheart, Kirby. For the first time in my life, I was all alone. But instead of dealing with those feelings of loneliness, anxiety, and stress, I ate. I ate and ate until I felt I had to throw up. I was purging up to twenty times a day. Each time I purged, I felt a sense of relief, a release of emotions—emotions I preferred to flush down the toilet rather than actually feel. But soon after, I would experience an emptiness that I would try to fill back up with food. It was a cycle that kept me spinning into a downward spiral.

Over the years, I managed to keep my eating disorder

under control enough to get through the rest of college, become a nurse, get married, and have two children. No one knew for almost ten years, but in 1983, my secret was finally exposed. To please my husband and my family, I went into treatment for three months and white knuckled my way through. But I hadn't committed to recovery for myself— because I wanted to get better—and I quickly relapsed. By 1988, my bulimia—and my life—was anything but in control. The strain of my eating disorder was beginning to affect my two boys, and my marriage had fallen apart. My weight had dropped below one hundred pounds, close to ninety. Our home was no longer a happy one.

My husband Bill and I decided to separate. I moved into a house just a few doors down the street. That way we could still have our time with the boys and work on our individual issues. Every other week, the boys stayed with Bill. This was really the first time I had to live by myself, and I hated it. I was ashamed, heartbroken, and desperate to be with my children.

One lonely, tearful night it became too much to bear. I mustered up the little motivation I had left, picked myself up, and walked down the street to my old house. Although I was standing on my two feet, I felt like I was crawling. As tears dripped down my face, I knocked on the door. Bill opened it to find me slumped over, bawling, and begging him to let me come back. I'll never forget Bill's face that night. His eyes were filled with sadness and disappointment. I pleaded with him to let me in, to at least stay for the night. Bill wouldn't even let me through the door. I knew I was a wreck and I didn't totally blame him when he told me I couldn't come in. "Deb, you need to get some help," he said solemnly. "Go get the help you need and then maybe we can talk." He slowly shut the door. My face was still wet with tears. I was completely alone.

In despair, I turned to my place of hope and inspiration: the mountains. I signed up for an excursion with Outward Bound, a life-changing wilderness program. It was a two-week backpacking trip through the Holy Cross Wilderness Area that involved hiking, camping, and rock climbing. It was refreshing and energizing to spend time outdoors in my favorite place. Near the end of the trip, the group made a technical climb up a forty-foot edge of rock on the side of the mountain. I was a little anxious all the way up the boulder, and at the top, I felt real fear. I was terrified to repel down, not only because I was so high, but because my safety would be in the hands of the man who was belaying me. In order to repel down, I had to trust the belayer and give up control. This terrified me. I slowly, nervously lowered my feet down the side of the rock, my hands shaking and my heart throbbing. The group told me to stop worrying, to trust them, and to just "let go." It took me a few minutes, but eventually I opened my arms and looked up towards the sky. I floated down with my arms spread wide and by the time I reached the bottom, I had made a crucial decision. I was going to change my life.

Climbing the mountain that day with the Outward Bound group triggered my decision to go into treatment. It was my turning point. As I was repelling down, I had a moment of grace and something clicked. I thought to myself, "Why am I living like this? What am I doing to myself? I have lived a secret life and done things I am not proud of. I have lost my marriage and jeopardized my health. I can't live like this anymore. I'm done. I am ready to change."

When I got home, my divorce was made final, and a week later I signed up for treatment. This time I was fully committed. I was done being a bulimic and I was ready to live a healthy and happy life. I spent an entire year in outpatient therapy for my eating disorder. The program was incredibly intense, but I had made a decision and I was committed to my recovery.

I am happy to say that I no longer struggle with eating, bingeing, or purging and I have been in recovery for the past twenty years. When I look back on the painful time I spent living with an eating disorder, I'm disappointed that I didn't make the commitment to my recovery sooner. But I also know that we all come to things in our time and in our own way. I can say in hindsight, though, that the most important thing to do is make that decision—and the sooner you can do it, the better. Until you decide that you do want to make a change in your life and that you do want to accomplish more, you won't.

Wanting something isn't the same as deciding that you're going to go get it. Don't wait for twenty years to go by. Don't even wait until next year. Decide now. What do you want to make of your life? Do you want to live another day, week, or month hoping and wishing for something more, but continuing to do nothing about it? Do you really want to continue telling yourself that what you want is never going to happen or that it will happen later? "I'll start my new diet on Monday," you say. "I'll look at enrolling in classes next summer," you think. "I'll put aside that dream until the kids go away to college." What are you waiting for? You don't have to live another second wondering about where your life is going to go. Decide right now. What is it that you want to do, accomplish, or change in your life?

Make a commitment to yourself that you are going to act upon your decision. Commitment is not just an outward effort; it starts from within. You can set goals and resolutions and make all the promises you want, but if commitment is not rooted deep in your heart, you are bound to disappoint yourself once again. Before you can begin to make external efforts to change your life, you must have an inward conviction. When you commit to doing something, you are not simply interested in doing it; you will accept no excuses, only results.

## Committing to the Journey, Step 1: The Pros and Cons

I believe everyone can realize his or her dream. That doesn't mean, though, that you shouldn't look at the practical considerations of realizing your dream. You can only achieve your goals when you figure out how to navigate the obstacles standing in your way. That's why it's so important to lay out the pros and cons of your dream—or dreams. You may need to make several lists, one for each of the goals and dreams you have.

Let's say, for instance, that you are an accountant who wants to start a new career as a middle school teacher. The pros or the positive effects might include: more time with family, greater satisfaction at work, a heightened feeling of importance, less overall stress, and room for creativity. The cons (which may or may not be negative effects) would include: going back to school, taking out a loan or saving money, a short time of increased stress, job interviews, and a pay cut. Weighing these pros and cons will not only help you decide whether it's a goal you truly want to pursue, but will also help you develop your game plan if you do decide to go forward. Use the following exercise to look at both sides of the coin.

What is it that you want to do? (Start a new career? Publish a book? Start your own business? Take up a new hobby?)

_____

_____

_____

_____

_____

_____

_____

_____

**Pros:** List all the benefits you'll get if you make this dream come true:_____

_____

_____

_____

_____

_____

_____

_____

_____

**Cons:** List how the decision to pursue this dream (and its eventual realization) may create challenges in your life:

_____

_____

_____

_____

_____

_____

_____

_____

_____

_____

Now that you have your pros and cons laid out, look at them. Go through and put a star next to the top three or four biggest effects this decision will have on your life whether they are benefits or challenges. For example, you may have to take a pay cut to become a teacher, but your day-to-day happiness is more important to you than your income. Are there more pros than cons or vice versa? Do the benefits outweigh the challenges you may face because of this decision? Record your thoughts:

_____

_____

_____

_____

_____

_____

_____

_____

_____

## Committing to the Journey,
## Step 2: Saying "Yes" and "No"

This is a similar exercise to the pros and cons, but it digs a little deeper. In order to say "yes" to one thing, you often have to say "no" to another. Sometimes you say "yes" to things you don't really want to and then you end up having to say "no" to things you value. For example, if you wanted to quit your job and become a stay-at-home mom, you would be saying "yes" to your kids and "no" to your salary. Or perhaps you are a stay-at-home mom and you want to go back to school and start a career. You would be saying "yes" to a career and perhaps "no" to your family. Each opportunity may bring about more than one yes or no. Write down the ones that apply to the goal you listed above. List the corresponding no for each yes.

| YES!<br>What will your dream require you to say yes to? | NO<br>What will your dream require you to say no to? |
|---|---|
| | |
| | |
| | |
| | |
| | |
| | |
| | |
| | |
| | |

Now that you can see your yeses and noes, which ones are you willing to act upon? Consider which yes or no answers are short, temporary ones, and which ones are long-term ones. Are you willing to say "yes" to yourself and "no" to your spouse and kids for a period of time? Are you willing to say "no" to your current job and "yes" to going back to school? Are you willing to say "yes" to skinny jeans and "no" to happy hour drinks and appetizers every Friday afternoon? Are you willing to say "no" to yourself, or are you willing to say "yes" to your dreams?

## Committing to the Journey, Step 3: Completing a Commitment Contract

When you sign a contract, whether it is a marriage license, a car loan, or a mortgage, you are legally bound to keep your end of the deal. In order to hold yourself accountable, I'm going to ask you to sign a commitment contract. You do not need to sign the contract until you are ready and fully committed. Hopefully by now you have begun to decide what it is you would like to accomplish, to understand both the pros and cons of the goal, and to have a good grasp on the yeses and noes your goal will require. When you have made the decision to go forward and are inwardly and whole-heartedly committed, fill in the blanks, sign, and date the contract. Then share it with at least one person, such as a friend, a family member, a counselor or life coach.

# Commitment Contract

I, (your name) _____
hereby promise to _____
_____
(fill in with the big dream or goal you want to accomplish)
by _____
_____ (month, year, or specific date).

I believe that I can and will accomplish my dreams. I have made a decision and I promise to act upon it. I am committed to the journey and will do whatever it takes to reach my "summit." I realize that with this decision will come some challenges. The process may be long and difficult, but the end result is worth it to me. I may have to say "no" to some things, opportunities, or people in order to continue my journey. I have decided to say "yes" to my dream of _____
_____ and
I am committed to making it come true!

Throughout this journey I will: (Initial)
_____-celebrate my small successes along the way.
_____-set goals that are reachable, enjoyable, and fulfilling.
_____-honor my passions, my values, and my strengths.
_____-not make excuses or allow negative thoughts to impact my decisions.
_____-overcome physical, emotional, financial, and personal obstacles.

I have made a decision and I am fully committed to the journey.
Signed_____
Date_____

Congratulations! You are on your way to climbing your own personal mountain. Trust me, the view from the top will be well worth it! I have never been standing on top of a mountain and thought, "Wow, I wish I wouldn't have wasted all that time and energy." No matter how hard the mountain climb is, I am always overjoyed at the top.

I am excited for you to start your journey. You have completed one of the most crucial steps. You can be proud of yourself for finally making a decision and committing to it. Envision yourself at the end of your journey. How will you feel? Who will you have become? What will you have gained? Pretty exciting, right? Are you ready to start climbing?

*"Man does not simply exist, but always decides what his existence will be, what he will become in the next moment."*
- Viktor Frankl

## One Step Closer...

You are now headed in the right direction! Celebrate your small successes this week. You can be proud of yourself for deciding and committing to following your dreams. After you have shared your vision with someone, record who you talked with and how they responded or reacted. How are you feeling, now that you have made a commitment? What do you need to say "yes" or "no" to this week to act upon your decision?

---
---
---
---
---
---
---
---
---
---
---
---
---
---
---
---
---

Greg at Sunlight Peak

# Mapping Out Your Dream
## Gathering Your Equipment

*"When you know what you want,
and you want it badly enough,
you'll find a way to get it."*

\- Jim Rohn

# ᔥ *Chapter Three* ᔥ

Now that you have envisioned your peak and decided to commit to the climb, you must start gathering your equipment. You have already begun to get into the right mindset by focusing on your dream. Gathering the necessary resources will continue to excite you and motivate you to keep moving forward towards your goals.

Any experienced hiker knows that you can't just get off the couch, drive straight to the trailhead in your current outfit, and bolt up a 14er. And if you chose to anyway, you would quickly encounter some obstacles, whether it be blisters, altitude sickness, or a thunderstorm you are completely unprepared for. I know you are excited and ready to start moving forward, but there are essential supplies you need before you begin your climb. I want to ensure that you will reach the summit and be able to take in the view when you get there. If you are equipped with the necessary resources, your journey will not only be successful, but enjoyable as well.

Even though getting ready for a trip isn't the most pleasant part, it is necessary. I have actually grown to like this component of hiking because it brings back memories of sitting with my family and laying out all of our equipment. My mother and father taught my brothers and me about the importance of preparing for the journey. They always made sure we had the essentials along with a solid plan and a reliable trail map.

I can remember getting ready for a big trip out to Colorado. My brothers and I would begin to get excited at the very thought of the beautiful peaks and amazing wildlife we were going to see. But my father would always stay focused on preparing and gathering our gear. He would take out all of our camping equipment and sprawl it across the floor in the basement. This way we could account for everything we already had and then decide what we still needed. Meanwhile, my mother would make sure we understood where we were going and how we would get there. She would point out the trail on the map, and be sure we understood which route was best. She was always working behind the scenes to ensure our safety and wellbeing. Even though my mom didn't hike with us, it was as if we brought her along because we knew she was at home thinking of us and waiting for our return.

I now have a similar preparation ritual in my own home. When we need to spread out our hiking equipment, there is a pool table in my basement that comes in handy. When we are getting ready for a hike or a backpacking trip, my husband and I will lay out our fuel, headlamps, hiking boots, hiking poles, pots, pans, floor pads, sleeping bags, tent, toiletries, food, clothes, and whatever else we need. My father still partakes in this custom when he visits Colorado. When we pack our gear, we laugh and joke, reminisce about the past, and motivate each other for the upcoming adventure. The year we climbed Holy Cross, my dad even made a map of his backpack on which he drew all the compartments and labeled where each piece of equipment was, so he would be able to access them more easily on the trail. My mother still always asks to see our map. She'll go over the trail routes until she knows exactly where we will be and how we plan on returning.

You too, need to lay out all of your equipment. Once you can see which resources are already available to you, you will have a clear picture of the supplies you still need. This takes time and energy, but it is crucial to gather your supplies now, before you begin climbing. This way, when you encounter a "thunderstorm," or run into a "boulder field," you will have what you need to keep going.

## Mapping Out Your Dream, Step 1: Pack Your Backpack

Think about the goal or dream you want to accomplish. What resources do you need? For example, if you are going back to school you may need to apply for a loan, ask your spouse for help with the children or housework, and determine a place in your house where you can study quietly. Or maybe you want to start your own photography business. This may require signing up for a class, purchasing a new camera, setting up a website, and working on the weekends. Think about spreading out your "gear."

Let's use the example of running a marathon as the big dream or goal. Below are suggested resources that you might need in order to accomplish this goal.

| Financial Resources | People |
|---|---|
| Monthly fee for gym or running club membership<br><br>$ for running shoes and work-out gear<br><br>Marathon entry fee | Personal trainer<br><br>A buddy to run with<br><br>My dog |
| **Physical Environment** | **Personal** |
| Map out routes around town, mini-courses leading up to 26.2 miles | Positive self-talk<br><br>Determination<br><br>Healthy diet<br><br>Music to run to |
| **Tangible Items** | **Time** |
| New running shoes<br><br>iPod arm strap<br><br>Complete registration form for marathon | Training plan, such as:<br><br>Run 4-5 times a week increasing mileage and speed |

On the compartments of your pack, list any essential resources you think you may need.

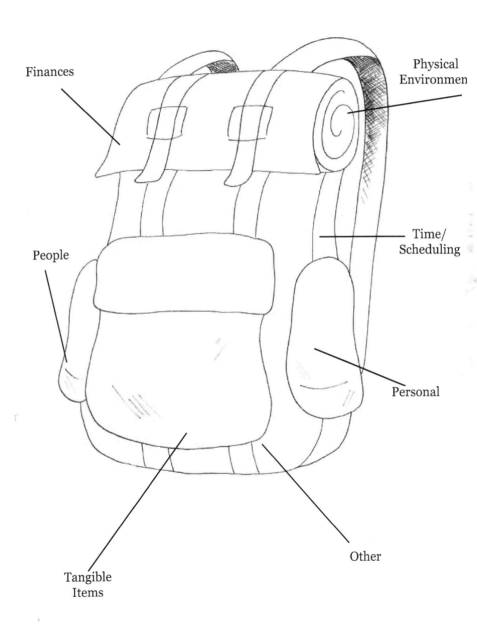

Finances

Physical Environmen

People

Time/ Scheduling

Personal

Tangible Items

Other

As a runner, you would need various resources in order to complete your first marathon. The same goes for any other goal you hope to accomplish. As you fill out the supply list for your particular dream, you may be as general or as specific as you need to be. Often with hiking, we pack, unpack, and repack. As you gather more information, resources, and come up with a concrete plan, you may need to rearrange the items in your pack. Some pieces of equipment should be easier to get to than others. Some items may just exist as a backup plan or in case you run into an unforeseen obstacle. Either way, it is always better to have what you think you "might" need, rather than not have access to it in a crunch.

Take a moment and look at your supply list. Which items do you already have available to you? Some items may simply be a request for help from a family member or friend, while another may require you to reschedule your day. Put a check next to the items you can access easily in your pack.

Once my family and I have spread out our equipment, we always discover a list of new items we need to purchase and ones we need to replenish from the previous year. We end up going back and forth to the grocery store and taking multiple trips to REI, the sporting goods store. Sometimes it is necessary to invest in new equipment, but often we make do with what we already have. In fact, for our trip to Holy Cross, I used my metal-framed pack from the 70's. And the year before, I was hiking in a pair of boots that were about eighteen years old. They were so worn the sole eventually fell right off as I made my way up the trail. I finished the hike with a foot wrapped in duct tape! To this day, we still sleep in an old, blue tent that I inherited from my family. Since it was made in the 60's it is much heavier than the new designs available today, but it still does the job!

Don't get caught up in having the latest and greatest of resources. When it comes down to a rainstorm in the middle of the night, my old tent serves its purpose. You don't need the newest, best, and most high tech equipment to make the climb. It's more important that you have the basic equipment. Beg, borrow, wheel and deal, or make do with what you have, just as long as you have your essential supplies.

## Mapping Out Your Dream, Step 2: Do Some Research

Next, you may need to do some research. Before my family and I ever set foot on a mountain, we do our homework. We research the trail, purchase a map, and find out the expected conditions of the trail and weather for the day of our climb. If there is going to be snow on the trail, we may need to pack items such as leg gators or crampons. If the trail conditions are unfit, we may need to explore another route on the map ahead of time. If a storm is coming in, we may schedule our hike for another day. We consider all the possible challenges we may face for that particular mountain and then we plan accordingly. If we didn't do this before our hike, we could possibly be putting ourselves in physical danger.

Look back at your supply list. Which items require more research? Perhaps you should look into a university program or class schedule. Maybe you need to read up on self-publishing or independent businesses. Could you meet with an expert in your desired field of work to find out more information? Record in the space below the specific areas you need to explore and the date you hope to accomplish this by.

| Area of Research | Goal Date |
| --- | --- |
| | |

Now you have a solid starting place. You have determined which resources you already have and ones you still need to gather. Consider the list of people in your backpack. Is there anyone else you can add to this list for support in accomplishing your big dream? Who in your life will you be able to rely on during the climb when the trail gets steep? Who will hold you accountable for accomplishing these goals?

# Mapping Out Your Dream, Step 3: Engage Your Support

My family and I have our own system for hiking. My husband, Kirby, and our son, Matt, usually take the lead. They set the pace and keep the momentum going for the rest of us. Next on the trail is Greg, leading the way in front of me. I watch his feet directly in front of mine. I place my feet exactly where his have just stepped, preventing me from tripping or stumbling. Stef follows behind me, her energy propelling me forward. Her voice motivates me to keep going as we dream up all sorts of ideas along the trail. This is the normal rhythm and pattern we fall into, however our order may shift and change depending on what we each need on any given hike. But if it weren't for my family, there are many mountains I would never have climbed— mountains in Colorado, as well as mountains in my life. When I have my support team surrounding me, I am able to climb even the steepest of peaks.

Who do you need to ask for support? How will you ask for their help? List specific names of people and how you will ask them for the specific support you need. For example, maybe you need to actually hire someone, such as a babysitter, to watch your children while you attend classes, an editor to assist you with your book, or a personal trainer to guide you during your workouts. You might need the support of a counselor or a life coach to help you plan out your dream. Maybe you plan to enlist the help of your friends, parents, or a mentor. In order for your journey to be successful, you will need at least one person who can provide you with encouragement each step of the way.

When my client Mark came to me, he knew he wanted to

make some serious changes in his life. At first he wasn't even sure what those changes should be; however, it was obvious to him that his life just didn't feel right anymore. During our sessions together we discovered that he had forgotten his passion for running and competing. To see if he could recapture the feeling, he registered for a triathlon and was soon on his way to his first event. But after a few weeks of training, we both quickly realized he needed additional support to reach his goal. That's when he made the move to hire more support, engaging a personal trainer that specialized in working with tri-athletes. With a personal coach to keep his life on track and a personal trainer to help monitor and steer his workouts, Mark easily tapped right back into his passion for athletics.

There will be times in your life when you need a lot of support, and there will be other times that the need for support will be minimal. It is key to recognize when you require that extra help, and then take the necessary steps to receive it. It doesn't necessarily mean you have to hire a professional; if that's not in your budget, turn to a trusted friend or family member and perhaps offer to do something for that person in exchange. In fact, if you have a service to offer, consider bartering with a professional, like a personal trainer or life coach in order to help you meet your goals.

List the names of people who could potentially help you in your quest.

| Name of Person | Specific support he/she can provide | When and how you will ask |
|---|---|---|
|  |  |  |

## Drive to the Trailhead

You have laid out your available resources and listed the ones you still need to gather. You have determined who will be a part of your support system and how you will rely on them throughout your journey. The next part involves arriving at the trailhead with your support team, your backpack filled with equipment, and taking the first step. The road ahead is a curvy one. This process rarely unfolds as a straight line. You may learn something new along the way or find another piece of equipment you didn't realize you needed. You may need to retrace your path or stop and ask for directions. However you get there, once you arrive, get out of the car and start hiking!

## One Step Closer...

After you have done some research, gathered resources, and arrived at the trailhead, record what you have learned. Which resources have you decided to invest in and when? Have you enlisted help from others? If so, how have they agreed to support you? Congratulate yourself for taking these actions and moving one step closer toward the trailhead. What are you most proud of accomplishing this week regarding your dream?

_____

_____

_____

_____

_____

_____

_____

_____

_____

_____

_____

_____

_____

_____

_____

Half Moon Pass
Mount Holy Cross
Deb, Greg, and Dad

# Taking the First Steps
## *Moving Past the Trailhead*

*"Take the first step in faith.
You don't have to see the whole staircase.
Just take the first step."*
- Dr. Martin Luther King, Jr.

# ∿ *Chapter Four* ∿

I love this quote on the preceding page. Dr. King's words are so simple, yet so true. All you have to do now is take the first step. Don't focus on the final destination, just put one foot in front of the other and move forward.

When my family and I are just on the verge of embarking on another 14er or backpacking trip, it's often the hardest part of the journey. We can be completely prepared, packed, and ready to go and still struggle when we reach the trailhead. Granted, we are more motivated to climb some mountains than others, but there is always some lag time when we first arrive. The scene usually unfolds something like this: We wake up in the early morning when it is still dark out. We start our drive towards the trailhead at least a half hour later than planned, and we yawn and moan for a good part of the way there. Some of us try to nap, but the bumpy, dusty dirt road usually prevents that from happening. We arrive at the trailhead an hour or so later. We all take a few minutes to sleepily gather our boots, pull up our socks, and tie our laces. Someone has to go to the bathroom and we all wait. Then someone else can't find something they need to get out of their pack. Another person is already complaining about the trail or the weather or the fact that we are getting started late again. We glance towards the beginning of the trail. There is a wooden sign with the name and height of the mountain and a posted number to represent the long, long distance we must travel. And this is how we begin our hike each and every time.

Taking that first step is always the hardest part. You can have every detail planned out and every piece of equipment you need. You could have trained hard and be physically and mentally ready for the journey. But until you take that very first step, you haven't actually made much progress towards your goal. Oftentimes we plan and prepare, but something stops us from taking the first step forward. In my family, we sometimes make a bunch of excuses: It's too cold. I've got too much to do this week. The weather might not hold out. I'm tired.

One time we were camping in Lake City, staying in a camper near the trailhead to Uncompahgre. We had planned to get up Saturday morning to hike the peak and then, on Sunday, hike Wetterhorn. We drove in late that Friday night and stayed up to organize our gear and prepare for the following day. We left our plans open for Saturday's climb, not really sure if we were committed to going. As we lay in our sleeping bags, we were all making excuses and whining about having to get up so early in the cold. Greg was experiencing the beginning of a horrible cold and Stefanie was stressed out about her job. I was exhausted. The next morning no one wanted to get out of bed. We got up an hour later than planned and took a long time to eat breakfast. Needless to say, we didn't make it to the trailhead until Sunday morning.

We were prepared and ready, but for some reason we couldn't get going that day. It doesn't matter if you have done all the research, all the packing, and all the planning. If you don't start putting one foot in front of the other, you can't reach your goals.

Think back to the exercises in Chapter 3. Have you enlisted support? Have you started your research? Did you fill out that application? Is your backpack stocked with the necessary equipment that you need? Remember you don't have to have everything ready. You don't have to have all of these things done. Just take one step. What is one small thing you can do to move towards your dream?

Often the reason we can't get started is because we look at the big picture—the whole "staircase"— and we get overwhelmed. Just look at that first step. When I am hiking I always look down at my feet. I focus on the ground that is right in front of me and then I place my foot there. Then I look ahead to the next patch of ground in front of my foot. I take another step. This is how I keep moving. When I look up and glance too far ahead up the mountain, I often get dizzy and lose my balance. I have to bring my focus back to my feet and just take one step at a time.

## Taking the First Steps, Step 1: Envision Your First Move

What is one small, doable thing you can start with? What is the first step on your staircase? How do you plan to get there?

_____

_____

_____

_____

_____

_____

_____

## Taking the First Steps,
## Step 2: Stop Making Excuses!

What are some of the excuses you have been making that have kept you from taking your first step?

_____

_____

_____

_____

_____

_____

What is overwhelming you right now as you think about climbing your mountain? What are you worried about? What is keeping you stuck at the trailhead?

_____

_____

_____

_____

_____

_____

_____

_____

What would it look like to have faith and step out onto the trail? How do you think you would feel?

_____

_____

_____

_____

_____

## Taking the First Steps,
## Step 3: Take Action!

Now you must follow the advice of Dr. Martin Luther King Jr. Go. Do. Act. Take your first step. Don't worry about the rest. Record what you did. List any thoughts or feelings that you experienced as you moved away from the trailhead.

_____

_____

_____

_____

_____

_____

_____

_____

_____

## One Step Closer...

Wow! You should be very excited and proud of yourself for taking action. You are well on your way up the trail! Sometimes when we move forward we experience opposition, fear, or other negative thoughts. Be aware of any negativity creeping in around you. Focus on the positive action you have taken this week and record the things you are proud of instead.

_____

_____

_____

_____

_____

_____

_____

_____

_____

_____

_____

_____

_____

_____

_____

Trailhead Sunshine Peak and Redcloud Peak
Stef, Greg, Deb, Matt, and Kirby

# Quieting the Voices Within
## *The Trail Gets Steeper*

*"Twenty years from now you will be more disappointed by the things that you didn't do than by the ones you did."*
-Mark Twain

# ≈ *Chapter Five* ≈

I was a nurse for thirty-four years. I spent the last twenty of those years in the G.I. lab where I assisted with repetitive, day-in, day-out procedures of colonoscopies and upper endoscopies. I literally felt like I was in a prison. There might as well have been bars on the doors. The G.I. room was a dark cell with no windows where I would work ten-hour shifts at a time. There was no way for me to use my gifts of intuition and creativity. The job was uninspiring, I had no passion for it, and it provided no opportunities to connect with others. I worked alongside one doctor on a sedated patient with a constant beeping heart monitor in the background. I found the G.I. lab was excruciatingly boring, senseless, and dreary. I received no real benefits or rewards from it, yet I continued to serve out my sentence for twenty years. I dreaded going to work every day. And during each grueling shift, as I watched the minute hand tick-tock its way from one hour to the next, I longed for something more.

"Well, why didn't you just quit right then and there?" you ask. But I couldn't! I was trapped! Something inside made it impossible for me to move. I told myself I was too old to make a career change and that it was too late. I should just stick it out and retire in another ten-plus years. I told myself I wasn't smart enough to learn new concepts, to pick up new skills, or to start a new career. It was too risky to start over now. Nursing and the G.I. lab was all I knew.

Defeated and depressed, I had decided I had no choice but to live and die in that dreadful lab.

Have you heard similar voices in your head? Negative self-talk, mind chatter, the inner critic? I call these internal voices the "saboteur." The saboteur can arrive in many different forms. It may, for instance, loudly announce its presence with obnoxious yelling and pounding in your head. This kind of saboteur creates so much noise that it pollutes your thoughts, making it impossible to think positively or clearly. Another type of saboteur is one who is subtle and sneaky, whispering quietly into your ear. Other times, the saboteur just sits heavily on your shoulders, not saying anything, weighing you down. However the saboteur emerges, it is a force that holds you back and tells you, "You can't do it." "You're not good enough." The saboteur clouds your vision, tramples your hopes, and infects your desires. You may not realize the saboteur's sly presence, but it keeps you from moving in the direction of your dreams. It may well be the reason that you have not yet accomplished your goals. I can say with certainty that it is the reason I was stuck in my G. I. holding cell repeating, repeating, and repeating mindless procedures day after day, year after year.

The saboteur was also the reason Jan, a 57-year-old woman who was married for over twenty five years, wasn't able to leave her marriage. When she came to me, she expressed how she had known for twelve years that the relationship was over. She and her husband were living separate lives without intimacy, love, or support for one another. Her saboteur played loudly in her mind, telling her all kinds of things like "You're too old to find love." "You can't support yourself on your own." and "The kids won't be able to handle it." Over time, Jan learned the tools and techniques for quieting the saboteur, which helped her realize that getting a divorce would ultimately bring more joy, happiness, and fulfillment to her life. She found the courage to stand up to those voices and filed for divorce a year later. On her own, she's realized that she's not too old for love, her children have handled the divorce just fine, and that she can support herself. The saboteur, in other words, was wrong.

So how do you stop those defeating voices? The first thing you must do is simply notice your saboteur. The saboteur can often go undetected, lurking around your subconscious. It will pretend to help you by disguising itself as a protecting force, offering to keep you safe from disappointment and failure. It wants to keep you right where you are, conserving the status quo. The saboteur will resist your movement towards growth and fulfillment, especially once you start climbing up the trail, further and further away from the trailhead.

You must learn to recognize your saboteur and then quiet its voice. Become aware of its presence and decide that you are not your saboteur, but rather its observer. Realize that it has no real hold over you. You can free yourself from its deceiving messages and have a life of joy, happiness, and fulfillment.

# Quieting the Voices Within,
# Step 1: Identifying Your Saboteur

*Recognize your saboteur's statements and strategies.*

The saboteur will say things such as " you can't," "you should," "you must," "you need to," "you don't deserve to." The saboteur loves to put you in a victim role or in a position where you can't make up your mind. Sometimes the saboteur will even convince you that you're about to die or going to die in the near future! (My saboteur always tells me this when I have to give speeches on stage or use a microphone at large workshops. So far, I have lived through it! My saboteur was lying!)

When I am hiking, my saboteur tells me that I am too tired, too weak, or that the trail is too dangerous. At the beginning when the trail is steep and I have not yet gotten into a rhythm, my saboteur is strong. I begin to focus on my aching muscles, on my heavy breathing, on my uncomfortable toes, or even on the long, long trail ahead. It would be easy to turn back at this point with the trailhead still in sight. I have to bring my focus back to the reason why I am on the trail in the first place. I recognize the voices and I tell them to go away.

What does your saboteur say? How does it announce itself? What strategies does it use to keep you from your dreams?

_____

_____

_____

_____

_____

_____

*Learn how the saboteur affects you energetically.*

The saboteur doesn't just speak to you; it affects your body and energy level. Paying attention to how you feel will help you become aware of the saboteur's doing. Common physical experiences from the saboteur may include loss of energy, agitation, tension, depression, anxiety, heat, weakness, restlessness, deadness, forgetfulness, tunnel vision, and numbness. When I was a nurse I suffered from horrible migraines and depression. My saboteur greatly affected my energy levels and my mood.

How does your saboteur affect you energetically?

_____

_____

_____

_____

_____

_____

_____

_____

_____

*Learn how the saboteur affects you emotionally.*

You may be more aware of your emotional responses than your energetic responses or vice versa, but it's important to pay attention to both. The saboteur may cause you to harbor feelings of guilt, sadness, inadequacy, fear, anger, shame, humiliation, isolation, lack of control, or hurt. It may convince you to think you are dumb, ugly, lazy, pathetic, or helpless. It may tell you that you are acting selfish, arrogant, or righteous.

My saboteur held me hostage to feelings of fear, anger, lack of control, and sadness. It allowed me to believe I had no choice but to stay stuck in my unfulfilling career.

What emotions have you felt as a result of your saboteur? What do your inner voices tell you to feel?

_____

_____

_____

_____

_____

_____

_____

_____

My saboteur went undetected for years before I was finally able to recognize its presence and its hold on me. Once I distinguished these voices and where they were coming from, I grew tired of listening to them. I hired my own life coach, which changed my life forever. Through the process of coaching, I was able to start quieting the voices of the saboteur and have the space to start dreaming and envisioning what I really wanted to do on this earth. And it turned out to be coaching. Today, I'm living the life of my dreams! I quit my nursing job in December 2008, and I can now say that I love what I'm doing. I have opportunities to use all of my gifts when I coach. My personal values are honored through my work. I have built a clientele, designed and presented workshops, and even led outdoor adventure women's retreats. These are things I never in my wildest dreams imagined I could do. I'm taking risks and growing every single day. I feel like the luckiest woman on this earth. And it's all because I was able to quiet the voices. I know from experience, it is possible to have the life of your dreams!

## Quieting the Voices Within, Step 2: My Saboteur's Biography

Write your saboteur's biography. This activity will allow you to recognize your saboteur and learn how it affects you. Try to include as much of the following as you can, regardless of your saboteur's comments. Have fun with it!

Describe your saboteur's physical representation, including its voice, stance, and attire. Does it possess male or female energy? Does it remind you of anyone? Maybe your saboteur reminds you of the snide girl in your high school geometry class. Maybe it looks like a family member who has always been dismissive of your goals or an annoying bird screeching in your ear. Perhaps it's completely otherworldly and appears to you as the devil or a werewolf.

What name or names does it go by? Give it a name if it doesn't already have one.

- List its habits when it is around you.
- What are its favorite sayings or stories?
- Write down its preferred circumstances for showing up.
- What are its skills and abilities?
- How does it hijack your values?
- What is its secret fear?
- What you do that gets it nervous, worked up, or otherwise on alert?

Describe your saboteur:

_____

_____

_____

_____

_____

_____

_____

_____

_____

_____

_____

_____

_____

_____

_____

_____

_____

_____

_____

_____

_____

_____

_____

_____

_____

_____

_____

_____

Draw a picture of your saboteur:

# Quieting the Voices Within,
# Step 3: Overcoming Your Saboteur

It is time to practice dealing with your saboteur. At my workshops and in my home office, I always hang a sign that reads "Saboteur, Out!" (I know, you just got acquainted and it's already time for your saboteur to leave!) Here are some strategies to try:

1. **Personify the saboteur.** This is a fun tangible way to work with the saboteur. You have already given it a name and identity and considered the type of energy it permits. Look at the picture of your saboteur. Who does it remind you of? What does it look like? When do you know it's around? Some examples of names I have heard for saboteurs are "Little Miss Know It All," "The Vampire," "The General," and "Naggy Nana." My daughter-in-law drew her saboteur as a charging bull with an angry face and smoke pouring out of its nose.

2. **Simply acknowledge the saboteur.** Talk to your saboteur, but take action in spite of its voices. Tell it to leave or move out of the way. Say things like, "Thanks for sharing, but I've heard way too much from you today. Its my turn now."

3. **Ignore the saboteur.** Don't interact with it. Just step over it.

4. **Give the Saboteur a job or a place to go.** Give your saboteur a task you don't like to do such as laundry, dishes, cleaning, or yard work. You can

visualize the saboteur doing these tasks, anything that keeps the saboteur out of your space. Or send it on a long trip to far away Siberia.

5. **Ask yourself if your values are being honored or dishonored.** We will touch on this more in depth in step 4, but for now think about which values are being dishonored because of your saboteur. How can you honor your values instead? When you choose to honor your values, the saboteur may disappear.

6. **Remember your vision or dreams.** When you remember and live in your vision, there's not any room for the saboteur. Revisit your vision board and notice how the saboteur's messages don't fit into your dreams or on your board for that matter. Hang a sign near your board with the message "Saboteur, out!"

7. **Separate from the saboteur.** What's the truth? Are the voices you are hearing truthful or are they false accusations? Don't allow the saboteur's lies to linger. Replace them with positive comments that are honest and respectful. To get rid of the voice of the saboteur, replace it with a mantra—a statement you say over and over to yourself. Jan, the woman I mentioned earlier who was stuck in a failed marriage used the mantra "I am capable, I am lovable, I can handle anything." As in Jan's situation, feeling as though you won't find love again, or be able to take care of yourself after years of being in a relationship, is a pretty normal response. While dating and finding a new love may not happen overnight, no one is ever too old to find love again, start a new career, or make a significant change in his or her

life. Your mantra might be, I can stand up to people who are disrespectful to me, or, I can learn a new skill, or, I don't have to say yes. Think about what the naysayer in your head has been telling you and take the opposite stand. When you pay attention to the confident voice in your head, you eventually begin to believe what you're hearing.

8. **Stay present.** Live in the moment and feel present through meditation, prayer, exercise, music, journaling, drawing, or relaxing. Partake in a creative activity such as writing or scrapbooking or soothe yourself with a cup of hot tea or a long bath.

## Quieting the Voices Within, Step 4: Clarifying Your Values

While I was working in the G.I. lab I was not honoring or manifesting my values. Boredom stood in the way of my creativity and my desire to be challenged. My sedated patients were unable to receive my intuition, inspiration, or deep soul connection. The lack of windows and natural light were an affront to my love for nature and denied my body's physical need for sunshine. The daily repetitive procedures of the job discounted my ability to learn and grow as a professional and disregarded my intelligence. I wasn't honoring my sense of adventure, love of the outdoors, and ability to create relationships. But once I stopped listening to the voices of my saboteur, I realized changing careers would allow me to manifest the skills and principles I had buried down deep in the G.I. lab.

Consider the things you value most in your life. Clarifying your values is not a decision-making process. Rather, it is a discovery—an unveiling of the values that already exist and are intrinsic to you and your life. Here is some guidance to help you clarify your values:

*Peak moments in time*

Look at snapshots of life when it was really good, rewarding and rich. Those fond memories represent times when a value (or values) that's important to you was being honored. For example, a friend of mine used to take volunteer trips to Cambodia every year. She loved working at the orphanages, spending time with the children, and feeling like she was giving back. These trips represented her values of community, giving back, and desire to contribute to the world. What are some moments like this in your life, and what do they represent about your values?

*Suppressed values*

Suppressed values are standards that you hold dear, but often ignore. For instance, one client of mine loaned money to a family member. While she knew it might be some time before she saw the money again, she was okay with the wait. But as the years went by, she became more and more resentful about the loan as she noticed the family member buying new things, and spending money in ways other than paying her back. When exploring this deeper, my client discovered that she didn't feel appreciated or respected, two important values in her life. Can you remember a time when you were particularly upset or angry? Look at the feelings that caused that anger. Now turn those feelings over and you will find a value that was being suppressed.

*Invisible values*

These are values you naturally or easily honor. Sometimes you are unaware you are even doing so; therefore you may not recognize them as values until something prevents you from honoring them. Do you, for instance, have a family member that loves to feed everyone who comes over to her home? Perhaps it is your grandmother or your mother. These types of people generally enjoy loving and giving to others, and when someone doesn't accept their kindness, their feelings are often hurt. You might even realize that you eat just to appease these generous types; essentially you are honoring their needs every time you do. That's an invisible value. Think about what comes naturally to you, and what you do without even considering it and expecting nothing back in return.

*Obsessive expression of values*

These values are being expressed in the extreme, becoming a demand rather than a form of self-expression. When you insist on something being "my way or the highway," there is a good chance there is a value being expressed in the extreme. This happens often in relationships. One of my clients, Betsy, came to me to improve her relationship with her husband. We started uncovering places where she was guilty of the "my way or the highway" thinking, such as when her husband wouldn't put his dirty dishes in the dishwasher, or would leave his dirty clothes on the bedroom floor. All of this drove her crazy and she was not accepting of her husband's transgressions. Growing up, Betsy always had to keep a clean room. Her father was in the military, and order was just a part of her family's dynamics. Although she values a clean home, and an orderly life herself, she realized that she was being extreme in expecting that in others. Eventually, she learned to compromise and found that she was much happier when she just let go of expecting others to be just like her.

*Must haves*

Look at what you MUST have in life. Beyond food, shelter, clothing, and other basics, what must you have in your life in order to be fulfilled? There will be a value there. Andrea, a client and colleague of mine highly values freedom. Anytime she is put in a situation where her freedom is compromised, she can feel the tightness in her throat, and immediately wants to break away. For years, she had countless jobs where she always felt trapped—simply because she had a rigid 9-to-5 schedule. Honoring this value, she learned that it was best to be self-employed and create her own schedule. Andrea also learned that it was best to always allow other people in her life the freedom they craved as well.

Record your thoughts:

_____

_____

_____

_____

_____

_____

_____

_____

_____

_____

_____

*What is a value, anyway?*

The following is **only a partial list of values**. There are hundreds, maybe thousands of values. We all share some of the same values; we just prioritize and articulate them differently. Feel free to add any of your own that are not on this list. Which ones are representative of your own values? Choose those that resonate most in your life, and then pick the top eight. Rate each value on a scale of 1 to 10 as to how well you are honoring each in your life.

| | |
|---|---|
| Accomplishment/Results | Directness |
| Accuracy | Emotional Health |
| Achievement | Excellence |
| Acknowledgement | Environment |
| Adventure/Excitement | Fame |
| Aesthetics/Beauty | Freedom |
| The Arts | Fun |
| Altruism | Harmony |
| Autonomy | Honesty |
| Authenticity | Humor |
| Being Challenged | Integrity |
| Clarity | Intimacy |
| Commitment | Independence |
| Community | Joy |
| Completion | Justice |
| Connection/Bonding | Leadership |
| Creativity | Loyalty |
| Certainty | Nature |
| Calm | Nurturing |
| Collaboration | Orderliness |
| Choice | Peace |
| Comfort | Personal Growth |
| Contribution | Patriotism |

Productivity
Positivity
Passion
Participation
Partnership
Power
Privacy
Relaxation
Recognition
Respect
Risk Taking
Romance
Security
Self-expression
Success
Sensuality
Service

Spirituality
Trust
Truth
Tranquility
Vitality
Validity
Zest

Others:

_____
_____
_____
_____
_____
_____
_____

Which value, would you like to be honoring more in your life?

_____
_____
_____
_____

What are one or two things you could do to honor this value more in your life?

_____
_____
_____
_____

How well are your values aligned with your current job, position, or life situation?

_____

_____

_____

_____

The beginning of the trail is often very difficult. You can still see the trailhead and easily turn back, get into the car, and go home. The saboteur is at work creating lies and trying to convince you to just give up. "You won't make it to the top," it whispers, "so why take another step?" You know otherwise. Your body is weak and the trail is steep. Your breathing starts to get harder and your feet feel cramped in your boots. Beads of sweat emerge onto your forehead. But you ignore the voices and you keeping putting one foot in front of the other. Right foot then left foot. Breathe in, breathe out. And you keep going. Because you are someone who climbs mountains.

*"Whether you think you can or think you can't, either way you are right."*

–Henry Ford

## One Step Closer...

What is the most critical, annoying message your saboteur tells you? What are two things you will do to quiet the voices within? How will you honor your values from now on?

_____

_____

_____

_____

_____

_____

_____

_____

_____

_____

_____

_____

_____

_____

_____

_____

_____

_____

_____

_____

_____

_____

Matt and Stef at Sunlight Peak

# Gathering Your Support
## *Sheltered by the Trees*

*"To acquire love...fill yourself up with it
until you become a magnet."*
                                                    –Charles Haanel

# ∼ *Chapter Six* ∼

You've been hiking for a while. By now the trailhead is long gone from your view. You've managed to find a rhythm in your breathing and a pacing for your steps. Your body has adjusted to the heat, your lungs to the deep breaths, and your legs to the physical exertion as you propel yourself up the trail. Your pack has settled itself onto your shoulders. Beads of sweat cool your skin as they trickle down your back. Your feet have finally become accustomed to the snug fit of your boots.

The trees surround you like a safe haven. They stand tall, ready to protect you from the sun's hot rays, from the wind's harsh breeze, or the wet cold rain. They come up alongside you as you make your way through their path. Their trunks are strong and sturdy, perfect for leaning on in times of rest. They are spectators on the sidelines, applauding your achievement. You can no longer see the summit of the mountain or even much of the trail ahead, but you trust the direction of the trees and you continue. You feel safe, supported, and alive. You are energized and refreshed. You know there are many more miles to climb and many difficult obstacles to come. But, for now, you are sheltered by the trees.

\* \* \*

In this journey to reach your personal peak, it is crucial to have some support. Like a weary hiker, you too need some guidance, protection, and encouragement. Think back to Chapter 3 when you were gathering your equipment. One assignment was to hire your support team. This week you will continue to develop this network of people who will encourage you to pursue your dreams. It makes the hike so much more enjoyable when you have the company of others and a little shade now and then from the trees. It is important to gather support now, before you are too high on the mountain and before you run into bad weather or giant boulders. This way, when you do reach that boulder field or when dark clouds roll in, you will be able to rely on your support to keep you going.

## Gathering Your Support,
## Step 1 : Ask for Help

Glance back to page 71. Whose names did you record? Which people did you actually take the initiative to ask for help? Are there people you still need to contact? Are you allowing yourself to receive their help?

_____

_____

_____

_____

_____

_____

_____

Think about the last question above. "Are you willing to receive help?" Sometimes allowing someone to help you is very difficult. It's easy to get stuck listening to those awful voices: "I don't really need help. I can do it better myself."

"I don't have the time or money to receive their help." "I will look weak if I ask for help." "I don't deserve the help." And so on.

Let me tell you about a time when I learned about asking for help and receiving support. There have been many times during my hiking experience when the trail has crossed over a babbling brook, a beautiful stream, or even a small creek. These I can usually handle, but sometimes there are raging rivers and these terrify me to the point of paralyzing fear. There are three perfectly logical explanations for this fear. First is that there is usually a single log or rock on which you have to balance in order to cross over the rushing, wild river. Second is that the river is a stinging, numbing, forty-something degrees Fahrenheit. And third, did I mention the river rages rampantly downstream past giant, jagged rocks?

The summer my father turned eighty and we made the sojourn to Mount of the Holy Cross, there was such a river. It was at the bottom of Half Moon Pass, just around the corner from the base of the mountain where we would set up our camp. We were so close to completing our hike for the day; we just had to cross the river and walk around a few trees and we were there! But first, we had to make it across that roiling, frightening body of water. True to form, there was a single log strewn across the middle, but the river had gotten so high that the log was basically submerged in the thigh-deep, freezing water. And, oh yes, the river was raging.

Everyone proceeded to take their boots off, roll up their pants, put their packs high on their backs and walk across the river one at a time. We'd have to move very slowly since the bottom of the river was filled with sharp, slippery rocks which could easily cut our bare feet or cause us to slip. By the time we'd make it to the other side, not only might our legs be drenched, but they could be completely numb as well.

When it was my turn, everyone waiting on the other side watched as I fearfully put my feet into the freezing water. I started inching across the riverbed, hanging onto the log. But about halfway out, I stopped. With my fifty-pound pack throwing me off balance and the strong current below, I was afraid to take another step. I tried kneeling onto the log so my legs wouldn't be as deep in the icy water, but I soon found myself wobbling on top of the log with my pack threatening to summersault my body down the river. I became completely frozen, unable to move. My husband and the kids started yelling encouragement. "Come on, Deb! You can do it!" I tried to adjust my feet, but all I could do was hang onto the log for dear life, crouched on my knees, almost in a praying position. My pack was teetering above my head now, and I could picture my whole body plunging downstream to my death. My legs were losing more feeling by the minute, but there was nothing I could do. If I repositioned myself, I might topple over. If I turned around I might fall in. I was completely stuck!

After a few moments of sitting in this awkward position, it occurred to me that I could ask for help, which I did. In an instant my husband and my son came from each side of the river and literally picked me up off of the log. They carried me and my overly large pack to safety on the other side of the bank. All I had to do was ask, and help was at my side.

## Gathering Your Support,
## Step 2: Commit to Receiving Support

Asking for help in the river was a life and death matter. Your situation might not be as immediately perilous, but living an unfulfilled life is serious. Don't be afraid to ask for help from your family members, a life coach, friends, or other necessary people. Allow people to come alongside you like the trees in the woods. And don't feel you need to wait until you are at your wit's end; you can ask for support right from the start. Looking back, I should have asked for help as soon as we approached that raging river and not waited until I was stuck on a log.

Give two examples of instances when you asked for help and it was beneficial.

_____

_____

_____

_____

_____

_____

Give two examples of instances when you didn't ask for help and realized later that you should have.

_____

_____

_____

_____

_____

_____

Name two situations for which you will commit to asking for help? How will you receive that help?

_____

_____

_____

_____

_____

_____

Stopping along the way to ask for support and being willing to receive it could change your life forever. After my "near-death" experience in the river, I realized how important asking for help was. I hired a life coach when I returned from my Holy Cross trip and started working towards quitting my job as a nurse.

Once I established Summit Life Coaching and my clientele, I again had to ask for my family's support before I could quit the G. I. lab. I had taken a leave of absence for a few months and hoped I never had to return. When two months had passed, I started debating whether or not I should go back. I received a call from my boss who wanted to know when I was coming back. I couldn't give her a specific time. I told her I didn't know when my leave would be over. After the phone conversation, I started hearing those voices seep into my mind again. "Deb, you should go back to earn your retirement. You should stick it out; finish the job. Nobody likes a quitter." I kept debating and second-guessing myself. My youngest son, Matt, finally said, "Mom, why in the world would you go back? You just need to quit."

A few days later, my boss called again and told me they

were no longer going to hold my position at the G.I. lab. At first I felt relieved, but then I began to feel guilty and even worried. Matt again stated the obvious. "You know why you lost your position, right Mom? You couldn't make the call yourself and just tell them you were quitting, so God decided for you." He was so right! With the support of my friends and family, I was finally able to leave my nursing career and coach full-time.

## Gathering Your Support, Step 3: Saying "Yes" and "No" Some More

In order to say yes to your dream, you sometimes have to say no to something else. With the help of my support system I was able to say no to nursing and yes to myself. In fact, I was able to say yes to a lot of things. Saying no to the G.I. lab meant yes to my coaching career, to working from home, to helping people, and to finally feeling content in my life. In Chapter 2 you made a list of yeses and noes. Revisit this list. Reflect on the following questions and record your thoughts.

Which items have you taken action upon and said yes to?

_____

_____

_____

_____

_____

What has this required you to say no to?

_____

_____

_____

_____

_____

_____

_____

How will this allow you to reach your goals or dreams?

_____

_____

_____

_____

_____

_____

Which items do you still need to say yes or no to in order to keep moving forward?

_____

_____

_____

_____

_____

_____

## Gathering Your Support,
## Step 4: Don't Get Stuck in a River!

Some of us find it easy to delegate tasks and share responsibilities. However, some of us find this difficult. This week you are going to ask for help. You may find yourself in the middle of a raging river, and you will need your support system to come over, lift you up, and carry you across.

Pick one of the people you listed in the exercise in Chapter 3. Get a piece of lined paper, stationary, or open your computer. You are going to write a letter to that person asking for the specific help you need. You may simply be writing a letter to your husband or to your child asking for their emotional support and understanding. Or maybe you have more specific terms for them to abide by, such as going to bed on time or helping around the house when you are busy doing homework for your master's class.

Maybe you need to write to a mentor, such as a friend, counselor, or life coach and ask for their advice. Ask this person to hold you accountable. Have them check in with you on your progress. Be sure that they will not allow you to give up and that they will celebrate in your success. Be sure they are willing to pull you out of the creek when you are stuck! Ask for encouragement, accountability, and whatever else you may need.

Whomever you chose, you need to complete the letter and deliver, mail, or send it to them by the end of the week. Don't wait too long ... otherwise, your toes might start to freeze while you're stuck on that log!!!

*Put a check in the stamp once step 4 is complete.*

*I have written and delivered/mailed my letter.*

As I have mentioned in earlier chapters, my family and I have a system for how we hike. When we are on the trail, we each take our place in front and behind someone else in the group. We propel each other up the mountain with encouragement and support. Sometimes, one of us may need a little persuasion, a little push, and some motivation to keep moving forward. At other times there may be a need for guidance; an example of where to place a foot, how to get around a boulder, or what decision to make about the weather. There are times when one of us may need to be comforted after facing our fears on a steep climb, protected from falling rocks, or applauded after a victorious ascent. My family and I support each other on the mountain and off. I can't imagine what might have happened if I wouldn't have had them there to pull me off the log and out of that rushing river.

## Gathering Your Support,
## Step 5: Visualize Your Support System

Think of all the people who have been supportive during this journey. Who have you gone to for help, advice, relief, encouragement? Who makes up your support system? You may have already listed their names in Chapter 2, but now I want you to see the support that exists around you. You are going to draw yourself in the middle of the trees, in the middle of all the people who are cheering for you. Visualize this image when you are frustrated, tired, or discouraged. Know that you are not alone. Store this image somewhere safe in your mind, or come back to this page to look at it. This picture will be an important reminder when you get to the boulder field, when you struggle up the steepest part of the mountain, or when bad weather is on its way. (Don't worry if you're not artistically inclined. Simply draw faces or people among the trees or write their names on each tree trunk or in its branches and leaves.)

Continue your journey along the mountain's path. You are reaching deeper into the forest, closer to your dreams. Notice the trees all around you. It is calm and quiet here. The voices are gone and you are free to enjoy the beauty around you. Welcome the cool shade that the trees provide as you pass by one after another. Their limbs overlap each other, forming webs of branches with little patches of light shining through the in-between spaces. As you steadily move forward, the sun winks at you through these spaces, causing your eyes to squint back. You breathe in the fresh scent of dew on the forest floor and the smell of the outdoors.

You do not have to be alone in this place. Allow others to enjoy this moment with you. Request support from your family, from your friends, or find a mentor or coach. Let them come alongside you to encourage you, to motivate you, to celebrate with you. Like the sturdy trees of the forest, lean on them when you are tired, frustrated, or confused. They will keep you going when the trail becomes difficult. Receive their support and enjoy their company as you continue your way up the mountain.

*"Let us be grateful to people who make us happy; they are the charming gardeners who make our souls blossom."*

-Marcel Proust (French Novelist)

## One Step Closer...

How did it feel to write a letter and request support? What response did you receive from the recipient? Were you able to begin receiving his or her help? How are you progressing towards your goals?

Deb sheltered by the trees at Twin Peaks

# Staying Present
## *Stop to Smell the Tiny Tundra Flowers*

*"Life is full of beauty. Notice it.
Notice the bumble bee, the small child,
and the smiling faces. Smell the rain, and feel the
wind. Live your life to the fullest potential, and
fight for your dreams."*
-Ashley Smith

# ∿ *Chapter Seven* ∿

My favorite part of any mountain is the alpine tundra. This is the place just after the tree line. It is also the place on Mount of the Holy Cross where my dad decided to turn back. I remember everything about that moment. The path had begun to turn from grass to dirt and then to rocks, and the trees seemed to have suddenly disappeared. Only the tiniest flowers and plants flourish in this land. In the wide clearing, I could see the bright blue sky, the puffy white clouds, and the tips of the other mountain peaks. As my dad turned around and began to walk back down the trail, I felt vulnerable and exposed much like the vast open field. I had to carry on without the comfort of my father's presence.

In the late spring and early summer this tundra is breathtaking with its magnificent blooms of bluebells and tiny daisies. These little patches of flowers and moss are reminders to stop and take in the beauty of the mountain; to stay in the present moment. The loveliness and openness of this place is inspiring. You feel free and at ease. Here you begin to realize how high up you are and how far you have come. Your body is tired, your feet are weary, but you know now the summit is just a little farther.

On this part of the mountain, there is always a shift, not only in the change of landscape but in your mindset. There is no longer a clear, marked trail. Now you have to look for the tiny rock statues called cairns, which will mark the trail for the rest of the way. And you no longer have protection or shade from the trees. Here, you are exposed in the wide open space, but you can also see more clearly. The summit may come back into view and you can almost touch the clouds. Here, you can appreciate your progress. You have come such a long way. The rest of the path looks steep and indistinct, but you are so close. Before you ascend towards the peak, stop to take it all in. Pause and remember the journey that brought you here. Take deep breaths, listen to the sounds, and bend down to smell the pretty little tundra flowers.

## Staying Present, Step 1: See the Beauty around You

Pick out three things in your day that are beautiful. Take time to notice and appreciate them in the moment; then, when you get home, jot them down in detail here or in a journal.

1. _____

_____

_____

_____

2. _____

_____

_____

_____

3. _____

_____

_____

_____

## Staying Present,
## Step 2: Savor Something

Stop to savor something today. Stay in the shower for a few extra seconds, or take a moment to appreciate the smell of your morning coffee before your first sip. Try to elongate the pleasant moments of your day, no matter how small. Write down a few simple treasures you enjoy to stop and savor throughout your day.

_____

_____

_____

_____

_____

_____

_____

_____

_____

_____

I can remember vividly the first time I put on a workshop. I was building clientele and loving my new job as a life coach. But if I was going to really make a career out of life coaching, I would have to take my business to the next level. I needed to gather more clients and build credibility and experience. I decided the next step was organizing workshops and retreats. This terrified me. I have always had an extreme fear of speaking in front of people, maybe even more so than crossing raging rivers! I knew I was going to have to work through this fear if I was truly going to be successful.

The first workshop I arranged was a vision board workshop. Each year, on or around New Year's Day, I

127

make a vision board for the year. It is a collage of my hopes, dreams, and goals. To represent my audience for my first workshop, I put the number 25 on my vision board. I would somehow pull in 25 people and I would somehow speak in front of all of them.

I started advertising, hanging flyers, and spreading the word for my workshop. People began signing up and, although I was nervous, I was starting to get excited. I had five people, then eight, then ten. By the week of the workshop, I had 12 attendees. I was a little disappointed. I had really expected my audience of 25.

The time came for my presentation and I was shaking in my boots. But I knew I couldn't let my nerves take over if I wanted these people to become future clients. I focused on each person who was sitting in the room. I picked one person to make eye contact with and I gazed at all of them, one at a time. I stayed in that moment and focused on my audience, connecting with each of them as individuals. I ignored the voice of my saboteur, the one that had told me in the past that I would mess up, stumble, and make a fool of myself. I stood in front of those twelve people, sharing my story, allowing myself to be vulnerable. In return, they were each willing to be open and to share their fears, hopes, and desires as well.

It was just like walking through the alpine tundra. There is often great risk to wind, weather, or even lightening in this place. But once you step out in faith and look around, there are beautiful sights to be seen. It is a scary experience to be vulnerable to others, whether it's related to your work, or to your personal life. But if you don't step out into the openness and take that risk, you may never see who you truly are, and you may never know your full potential. If I had never done that very first workshop, I wouldn't be where I am today. And you would not have this very book in your hands. Looking back on my coaching experiences, that first workshop was one of my favorites. I was so aware of myself and of the people in the room. I was learning through each moment of it. I didn't die, or faint, or make a fool of myself. I was able to feel proud and accomplished. I received very positive feedback that day, and my clients returned. I embraced my fear of public speaking, and my workshops now come second nature to me.

I put on another vision board workshop just a few days after the first one. When I counted the number of people who were signed up, it was 13. Then I realized 12 and 13 makes a total of 25! If I hadn't stopped to be grateful for the clients I gathered for each presentation, I wouldn't have been able to see that total number and appreciate what actually came true. You might not always accomplish your goals exactly how you envisioned them, but chances are, if you take the time to look around and sum up what is really there, you will see that you did indeed make strides and that your accomplishments, even the tiniest ones, are something to be proud of.

## Staying Present,
## Step 3: Express Gratitude

I have a wonderful quote on gratitude that I refer to in my workshop Crossing the Bridge from Burnout to Bliss:

*"Gratitude unlocks the fullness of life. It turns what we have into enough, and more. It turns denial into acceptance,*

*chaos to order, confusion to clarity. It can turn a meal into a feast, a house into a home, a stranger into a friend. Gratitude makes sense of our past, brings peace for today and creates a vision for tomorrow."*

-Melody Beattie

The road to success is not often an easy one. A little gratitude can change your outlook entirely and provide you with enough energy to keep going. When I am in the tundra, I am grateful for the tiny little flowers, the green moss, and the fresh open air. Appreciating the mountain and its beauty supplies me with that little "oomph" I need to make the final push towards the summit. Here are some ways you can express gratitude for the little things in life.

Ideas for Expressing Gratitude:

- Sinking into a warm tub.
- Two hours in a bookstore.
- Watching the sunset.
- Acceptance after struggle.
- Meeting a deadline.
- Uninterrupted sleep.
- The first morsel of your favorite comfort food.
- Moving on.
- Air-conditioning on an excruciatingly hot day.
- A nice warm cozy fire.
- Perfect timing.
- Writing a thank you note or letter.
- Prayer or meditation.
- Completing a crossword puzzle without help.
- Listening to oldies and recalling happy moments.

## Stay Present,
## Step 4: 10 Fingers, 10 Toes

Gratitude is powerful. Most days when I wake up, I try to start my day by counting the things I am grateful for on each of my fingers and toes. It may be as small as the two minutes I have left to stay in bed, or as big as having a job I love. Tomorrow when you wake, before getting out of bed, count one thing you are grateful for on every finger and every toe.

## Stay Present,
## Step 5: Be Inspired!

What is something you love to do, something that allows you to feel inspired or to be creative? Sign up for an art class, go on a hike, take pictures, or spend time journaling, drawing, scrapbooking, knitting, or baking. Go dancing, spend time in nature, take a yoga class, or make music. Allow yourself to create, enjoy, and savor the moment. Whatever you choose, take time this week to honor your values by doing something you love. Or try something new. Maybe there is something you have always wanted to do, but you were too afraid or too busy. Put yourself out there and see what you learn from it. At the end of the week, record what you ended up doing and how it inspired you.

_____

_____

_____

_____

_____

# Stay Present,
# Step 6: Self Care

In life, we often neglect the care and concern of ourselves. You may be too wrapped up in your job, your family, or even in reaching your goals to stop and care for yourself. Yes, you can even get burnt out on the people and things you love! It is important to stop every once in a while and enjoy the finer things in life, no matter how small. This week, schedule at least one act of self-care. Allow yourself to rest, relax, or take joy in a soothing activity. Which value of yours needs honoring? What is one way you could honor it through self-care? Below is a list of ideas to help you get started. Try one this week and then decide which ones you can regularly work into your life in the future.

*Suggestions for Self-Care*

In the Workplace:

- Develop your own brand of happy hours, celebrations of birthdays, or other events as a break in the routine.
- Be clear regarding what is expected of you and ask for feedback.
- Ask yourself if your identity and self-worth are wrapped up in your work activities or work roles.
- Determine if tasks or projects can be shared or if parts of them can be delegated to others (both at work and at home).
- Take breaks. Walk around, stretch, practice conscious breathing. Don't take your job with you on breaks. Go outside, and into the sunshine.
- Keep reminders or objects at your desk, such as a

smooth stone, a bible verse, a meaningful picture, or an inspirational quote. These can help reduce stress and bring perspective when needed.

- Play quiet music in your office, or use scented candles or heated essential oils to keep you calm or cheerful.

General:

- Plan ahead whenever possible, so as not to create additional stress when the unexpected occurs.

- Whenever possible, un-do mistakes immediately, so you don't have to deal with them later, when they may be harder to face.

- Develop a wider variety of sources for gratification in your life. Make changes in your interactions with family and friends and expand your hobbies and interests.

- Don't overlook the emotional resources available to you close at hand: coworkers, supervisors, friends, and family.

- USE HUMOR, whenever possible. Consciously look back at the end of your day, and remember the laughing that you did and shared.

- Plan fun activities or mini-vacations, so you always have something to look forward to.

- Spend time in nature.

- Purchase your favorite fresh flowers for your home or office. It may brighten your whole day and put you in a cheerful mood.

- Meet a friend for coffee and catch up.

- Schedule a date night and have someone else watch the kids.

- Exercise or find some form of movement you enjoy. Take a short (or a long) walk.

- Get cozy in your favorite chair or on the couch and read a good book or watch a movie.

- Engage in soothing activities such as a massage, warm bath, or cup of hot tea.

- Take a "music bath." Find a comfortable spot, pick out your favorite song or piece of music, turn off the lights, close your eyes, and *listen.*

- Record your successes in a journal or on a note card.

- Keep a gratitude journal and write about the positive parts of your day, focusing on what you appreciate in your life.

- Spend time praying, meditating, or just simply being still.

*Commitments for Self-Care*

What two self-care activities will you implement into your life?

_____

_____

_____

_____

_____

_____

_____

How will you accomplish this?

_____

_____

_____

---

---

---

---

Enjoy this time in your journey. Stop and appreciate what you are learning and how far you have come. Don't be too focused on the final product or outcome. Stay in the present moment by honoring your values, practicing self-care, and expressing gratitude. Allow yourself to be vulnerable and examine why you are working towards this goal. Celebrate your small successes, and look back on your journey thus far. See all the pretty blooms around you, and breathe in the fresh air. There is still a challenging road ahead, and there may be storms on the way, so gather a little gratitude here and some inspiration from over there, and put them in your pack for later. When you are ready (once you have taken a moment, taken in the view, and snapped a few pictures), take a deep breath, face forward, and begin climbing again. The tundra is turning from rocks to boulders, and they are getting bigger with every step. You can see clearly now, and you know exactly where you are going next. Bring on the boulder field!

*"The whole life of man is but a point in time; let us enjoy it, therefore, while it lasts, and not spend it to no purpose."*
- Plutarch (Greek historian and writer)

## One Step Closer...

You have been actively working towards your goal. This often takes hard work, time, and dedication. However, you have made progress! You can see the clouds overhead, and the summit is near. Record three things that have gone well during your journey. (They may be big or small things, but write down anything that has gone well and *why* it went well.) Example: I got a call back from a new potential employer; I downloaded the application for college/course; I hired a coach to get me back on track.

Greg smelling the columbines at Mount Democrat

# Overcoming Obstacles
## *Boulders, Storms, and Altitude Sickness*

*"Crisis is one-half danger
and one-half opportunity."*
-Donald Dohn, Neurosurgeon

# ≈ Chapter Eight ≈

My father has always said that crisis is "one-half danger and one-half opportunity." My children and the other grandchildren in our family know this saying of his well, and many famous people, including John F. Kennedy, Al Gore, and Richard Nixon, have stated different versions of this quote. I think perhaps Kennedy explained it best: "When written in Chinese, the word 'crisis' is composed of two characters—one represents danger, and the other represents opportunity."

Opportunity and danger do seem to come as a pair. When we take advantage of opportunities to accomplish great things, it can be dangerous. And when we find ourselves in dangerous situations, there are always opportunities lurking about. Often in life, it is not so much the situation you are dealt but how you choose to deal with it. Attitude is *everything*. Instead of seeing a tough situation as simply negative and difficult, look for opportunities—opportunities to learn, opportunities to grow, and opportunities to change. How might this difficult task or time strengthen your character?

Most of us tend to wait around for opportunity to come knocking on our door. It is safer that way. We'll just sit and wait comfortably in our own homes and when it knocks, we will answer. What if, instead, you went looking for it? Sounds dangerous? You are right. But think of all the people you know who have purposely put themselves into dangerous situations, the people who went looking for danger: Christopher Columbus who sailed all around the world and found something he wasn't expecting to find, America! Ruby Payne, the little African-American girl who walked to school each day through mobs of angry, hateful white people threatening her life and telling her to stay out of their schools. She changed public education in our country forever. Martin Luther King, Jr., who risked his reputation, his freedom, and ultimately his life for his dream of equality in our country. The list goes on to include Rosa Parks, Albert Einstein, Leonardo da Vinci, Gandhi, Mother Theresa, Mozart, Louise Braille, Alexander Graham Bell, and Charles Dickens. These are just a few people who dared to seek out danger and discovered amazing opportunities. There are so many sports stars, presidents, musicians, scientists, explorers, adventurers, and others who decided to get up, go out, and be "dangerous."

* * *

On mountains, there are many dangers and obstacles that pose potential threats to a successful summit. The first and most obvious obstacle is the weather, especially in Colorado. The summer days here can be deceiving. Even with an early start, clear blue skies, and not a cloud in sight, by early afternoon, you may be standing on the peak beneath a dreary black rain cloud looking at lightning in the near distance. Hail and sleet are not uncommon in the middle of July when you are near an elevation of 14,000 feet. And yes, even snow, along with drifty winds, may spoil your beautiful mountain experience. Then there is always the possibility of altitude sickness. This little distraction may include side effects such as: headaches or migraines, loss of balance, dizziness, fainting, nausea, vomiting, and dehydration. Even native Coloradoans are at risk for altitude sickness if they aren't physically prepared for hiking, or if they don't stay properly hydrated or eat enough.

What else? Oh, yes. Sometimes there are barriers that are more annoying than threatening, like squishy mud pools, thick brush or poky bushes, buggy swarms, muscle cramps, aching knees, wind burns, sunburns, or sweltering blisters from your boots. Sometimes you must cross raging rivers, snow fields, icy patches, giant boulders, narrow ledges, drop-offs, or scree (scree is a bunch of lose rock, often on a steep section of the mountain, which makes for easy slipping and sliding). These obstacles are not only physically challenging and dangerous, they may have a detrimental effect on your mind. You begin to imagine the "what if" and fear takes over. Fear then becomes a hindrance in itself, preventing you from thinking clearly, staying calm, and maintaining composure while you cross over these high-risk mountain zones. This may cause an increase in blood pressure, breathing, and adrenaline. It may even produce tears, which sting your face and blur your vision, adding yet another dangerous component to the adventure—"blind-hiking."

As you can see, there are just as many obstacles on a mountain as there are in life. "So why go through them?" you ask. It doesn't sound as fun as you had thought. But remember these obstacles can be viewed as dangers or opportunities. Danger on a mountain can be an opportunity to overcome fear. The same is true in life. Maybe you want to change your career. There are many dangers in this decision. Your finances may take a hit, you may have less time with your family while you are taking classes, and it could take a

REACH YOUR SUMMIT AND BEYOND

while to find a job in your new profession. Perhaps, though, this new job is something you would absolutely love to do. You may end up a happier, more productive person because of it. You may even become a better spouse, parent, and friend. The danger of changing your career could be an opportunity for you to use your gifts, an opportunity for your children to learn how to clean the house, an opportunity for your spouse to practice generosity, and an opportunity for you to learn how to ask for and receive help. Again, where there is danger, there is also opportunity. You just have to be willing to see the opportunities that are disguised as giant boulders, hail storms, and scary ledges. Crossing these obstacles can be risky, but what is on the other side is almost always worth the risk.

On mountains, my family and I hike to the top because after crossing all those hurdles and scary parts, we are able to enjoy the view. Each of us is able to look back and say, "Wow! Look how far I have come! I just covered all that ground? I went up that scree field? I climbed over and around those boulders? I made it past that scary ledge? I really did that?" When you reach the top, the feeling of accomplishment is completely rewarding. And the view is indescribably magnificent. When you stand on top of the mountain and you are higher than the rest of the world, it is all worth it.

## Overcoming Obstacles,
## Step 1: Danger vs. Opportunity

Life presents us with many hardships and struggles. At any point in time you may experience failure; feel loss, depression, or pain; experience disappointment, illness, injury, or heartache. You may struggle with family, friends,

144

money, jobs, health, and even time. And you can look at each of these troubles as a danger or as an opportunity. Think about what you've encountered along the way.

What obstacles are you running into during this journey to your personal peak? What has stood in your way, frustrated you, or hindered your progress? An obstacle could be a lack of resources, time, or support or a barrier that is actually blocking your advancement towards your dreams, such as fear, your mindset, your attitude, a person in your life, or a physical limitation. List them here:

_____

_____

_____

_____

_____

_____

_____

How can you look at these obstacles differently? Record the danger of the most threatening obstacles in the chart. Then next to it, write what type of opportunity you may be presented with because of this obstacle. (Example: Publishing a book is very expensive and time-consuming and therefore it could be a danger to your time and finances. It could also be an opportunity for furthering your professional development, improving your time management, learning about the publishing process, and increasing the success of your business.)

| Obstacle = | 1/2 Danger | 1/2 Opportunity |
| --- | --- | --- |
| | | |

What do you think you might learn if you overcome these obstacles?

_____

_____

_____

_____

_____

_____

_____

# Overcoming Obstacles,
## Step 2: Check for Altitude Sickness

Acute altitude sickness can occur as low as 8,000 feet, but your risk for this illness will increase as your elevation also increases. It occurs in up to 50 percent of people living at low lands who then ascend to 14,000 feet or higher. People who are at greater risk for developing altitude sickness are those who live below 3,000 feet, or those who rapidly ascend to high altitude. The most common symptoms are headaches, nausea, vomiting, and fatigue.

Altitude sickness is a metaphor for risks you face on your own journey. You are used to living in "low lands"— the place where you remain in the status quo. But lately you have been ascending, rather rapidly, up your personal peak. You are likely to experience some effects from this "high altitude." You may feel dizzy, unbalanced, or fatigued. You have been working hard to pursue your dreams, and at this stage of the game you may begin to tire out, lose focus, get stuck, or even stop in your tracks. Don't worry; about 50 percent of people do.

What symptoms are you experiencing? Put a check next to each that apply to you.

_____ I feel unmotivated, stuck, or unsure of the next step.

_____ I am tired of working on this project/goal/dream.

_____ I am bored.

_____ I frequently complain or whine to others.

_____ I don't know what to do next.

_____ My life is unbalanced right now; I am too busy.

_____ I don't have the confidence to move forward (the saboteur is creeping about).

If you have two or more of these symptoms, you are experiencing "altitude sickness"!

## Overcoming Obstacles, Step 3: Remedy Your Altitude Sickness

On the mountain, you can prevent altitude sickness by drinking plenty of water, moving slowly and steadily, and fueling your body often with energy-filled foods. In life, it's not all that different. You sometimes just need to slow down, take a short break, and recharge. Did you know it is possible to get burnt out on your dreams? I remember a bout of "altitude sickness" during my second year of coaching and organizing mountain retreats. I facilitated three outdoor adventure retreats in one year, and was even planning on doing a fourth. On top of the planning and gathering of clients for the retreats, I was coaching all day, every day. I started getting headaches and feeling overwhelmed and exhausted. Suddenly I realized that I could overdo this job, too. I ended up cancelling the fourth retreat, and thank goodness I did! I was doing way too much. Even when you love what you do, you have to find a balance and take the time to care for yourself. Here are some steps to take in that direction.

Do you need a small break from this project? If so, decide what actions you will fill your time with. Then enjoy a short, purposeful break, and set a time and day that you will return. This will allow you to recharge and keep you from getting stuck altogether.

I will fill my time by...

_____

_____

_____

_____

_____

_____

_____

_____

I will continue my journey on....

_____

_____

_____

_____

_____

_____

_____

_____

If you feel you don't need a break, do you need to be recharged and reenergized to keep going? What could you do to renew your energy and find inspiration? Who in your support network could you turn to for motivation or advice? Do you need to ask anyone else for help?

_____

_____

_____

_____

_____

_____

_____

_____

Which self-care and/or gratitude activities from Chapter 7 could you be using more often?

_____

_____

_____

_____

_____

_____

_____

_____

Is your attitude causing your "altitude sickness?" What negative thoughts, complaints, or messages have you been giving or getting?

_____

_____

_____

_____

_____

_____

_____

If your attitude is out of whack, this exercise may help: Change each negative response above to a positive one. (Remember danger vs. opportunity!) For example, one of your comments could be that you are almost done writing your book but you don't know if it is any good or if it is worth the hassle of publishing. Instead, tell yourself that you are almost there and that all you have to do is publish! You will be a professional author, and people are going to love your book! Record your newfound positive responses here:

_____

Lastly, you need some fuel from your pack to get around these boulders. What kind of "fuel" are you lacking in? Maybe you are not getting enough sleep, exercise, healthy food, time with family or friends, time to yourself, appreciation, or encouragement. What kind of "fuel" do you need more of?

_____

How or where can you get that fuel? What resources or people can you revisit to help you maneuver around any obstacles that may be blocking your way?

_____

\* \* \*

When I quit my nursing job there were many dangers. Being self-employed meant no benefits, no 401K, and an unsteady paycheck. I would be losing the security of a guaranteed salary, health insurance, and the benefits of a retirement plan. My husband was also running his own business, so our income would be dependent solely upon our clients, and the state of the economy. I knew as a life coach I would have to do more work upfront to constantly obtain new clients. There was no guarantee I'd succeed and no cushion for me to fall back on.

However, as a life coach I had the opportunity to make three times the amount of money I did as a nurse. Ultimately, my new endeavor provided me with enough funds to cover my bills, my insurance, and create a savings! I also had freedom over my schedule, and I was able to use my gifts doing what I loved each day. My physical symptoms from stress disappeared. My migraines stopped, and my attitude changed drastically. No more nights lying awake in worry. No more dreading the start of the next day. The opportunities of this risky career change far outweighed the dangers!

Yes, the opportunities were amazing, but wasn't I scared? Of course! That is why it took me almost thirty years to make a change. I had to overcome my fears in order to see what a great opportunity life coaching would be.

I often find myself in this same predicament on the mountain, especially since I hike with my sons and daughter-in-law, who seem to enjoy presenting me with great "opportunities." Most recently my son Greg wanted to hike the rock face connecting Mt. Bierstadt and Mt. Evans, two neighboring 14ers. Known as "the sawtooth," it is a bunch of craggy rocks dipping and pointing in between the two mountains. Had I known what an adventure my son was taking me on, I would have stayed home.

First we ascended easily to the summit of Bierstadt. Then, as we began down the first plunge of the sawtooth, I started wondering what I was getting myself into. We began to move slower and slower as we focused on careful foot placement around boulders and ledges. Boulder fields always make me a little more cautious, but this one was nerve-racking. Around each corner was a drop-off hundreds of feet down, causing us to have to turn around, re-route, and find a detour. We ended up moving around the boulders to take a more careful pathway, only to go back up them to make our way across the sawtooth. It was a grueling and tense hike. And then we reached the final and most threatening obstacle. The last hundred feet or so was a traverse around the steep face of the sawtooth. This side of the mountain was not a ledge of boulders. Oh no, it was all made up of scree, those small loose rocks I described earlier. And they were sitting all over the invisible trail that allowed you only a few feet on one side and a vertical wall on the other. Overhead making their way towards us were large, dark, puffy clouds.

So there I was standing on a tiny path with a precarious edge, scree to slip on, and weather to worry about. Not only did I fear for my own safety, but for my children's as well. In this moment, I knew I couldn't let my fear overtake me or I might add to the already dangerous situation. I simply had to turn off the fear, shut it out of my mind, and just move forward. I pushed the terror aside, hugged the mountain, and kept climbing. When I had made my way around the last corner, I breathed a huge sigh of relief! If I can avoid it, I will never climb another sawtooth!

The point is, your mind can become an obstacle in itself. We often come so far, only to tell ourselves we are not good enough, not prepared enough, or not worthy of our dreams. Don't allow fear to keep you from taking the final steps to your summit. Don't second-guess all of your progress and accomplishment. If you don't let go of your doubts and fears, you may never know what beautiful things you might discover around the corner!

## Overcoming Obstacles, Step 4: Face Your Fears

You are about to complete your journey and accomplish your dreams! This can be overwhelming and scary as well as exciting. What comments are you receiving from the saboteur? What are you most afraid of as you take the final steps to accomplish your goals?

_____

_____

_____

_____

_____

_____

_____

_____

_____

_____

_____

_____
_____
_____
_____

Give these thoughts and fears a place to go. Send them over the edge of the sawtooth or to a far off place!

## Overcoming Obstacles, Step 5: Climb Over those Boulders!

What is the next step or steps you must take to accomplish your dream? What are the final things you need to do?

_____
_____
_____
_____
_____
_____
_____

Remember, you can stop for a little while and take a short break to recharge, but don't forget to stay focused and to keep going. You are so close! Return to your commitment contract in Chapter 2. Have you kept the promise you made to yourself at the beginning of this journey? Review the date you recorded on your contract. How close is that date? Will you be able to meet this expectation? If not, record a new date that is more realistic:

_____
_____
_____

Though most mountains do not have anything as dangerous as a sawtooth, there is always a boulder field. There might not be bad weather, or scree fields, or any other significant problems, but there are always boulders during the final parts of the trail leading up to the summit. On this section of the climb, you must change your rhythm, your way of movement, and your thinking. This part requires a deeper focus, a slower pace, and careful attention to where and how you place each foot and hand. This part of your journey requires a lot of energy and meticulous movement. If you have not had enough water or food, if you are not alert and strategic, you may trip, twist your ankle, or scrape yourself on a sharp boulder. Even so, it is too late to turn back now, for the road back is much farther than the one ahead. And you cannot stop too long on this area of the mountain. You are exposed, weather could creep in, and you do not want to lose your focus. It is only a little bit further. You are nearing the final push. Stop and breathe, drink water, eat a snack or two. And then take the next step. And then the next, and the next. The summit is just within your reach!   Dare to overcome danger!

*"We are all faced with a series of great opportunities brilliantly disguised as impossible situations."*

- Charles R. Swindoll

## One Step Closer...

Think back on your life to a time when you overcame some type of struggle. It could have been the loss of a job, the death of a family member, or a frustrating illness or injury. How did you get through it? What opportunities were presented to you? What did you learn from that experience? How could you use what you have learned from life's obstacles to help you now?

_____

_____

_____

_____

_____

_____

_____

_____

_____

_____

_____

_____

_____

_____

_____

_____

_____

Deb and Stef in the boulder field
at Mount Lady Washington

# *Dealing with Disappointment*
## *False Peaks*

*"Disappointment to a noble soul is what cold water is to burning metal; it strengthens, tempers, intensifies, but never destroys it."*
-Henry Ward Beecher

# 〰 *Chapter Nine* 〰

In mountain terminology, there is something called a "false peak" or "false summit." This is the part of the mountain that makes you think you have finally reached the very top—only to discover that you haven't. It looks like the summit, it feels high enough to be the summit, and you really wish it was the summit, but it is not the actual summit. When you are hiking, you can't see anything beyond it and you don't realize until you are on top, that there is much more climbing to do. And if you wish to really be at 14,000 feet, to be at the highest point on the mountain, then you must keep going. These false summits are so disappointing! Many 14ers have them, some even three or four. The disappointment lies not only in the fact that you were just building up excitement for the peak and now you realize you are not on the peak, but also in the fact that you are so tired and worn-out, and now you have to muster up *more* strength and energy to make *another* steep push to the *real* summit.

When I began my journey to become a life coach, I experienced a similar type of disappointment. It was so disappointing and embarrassing to me that I have been debating whether or not I should even share it with you. I mean, do you enjoy admitting your mistakes and embarrassments? I didn't think so. But for the sake of this chapter, and keeping in mind the fact that I am indeed a human, I will share my story.

In order to become a life coach there were many courses, evaluations, and observations I was required to pass. I also had to pass a final oral exam. These types of words—"test," "assessment," and "exam"—have always made me nervous. But I had passed the boards in nursing school. Surely I could pass my life coach exam.

I first had a series of evaluations. My supervising coach was required to observe me coaching a client several times. Though I was nervous, each time I performed exceptionally well. My scores on my coaching sessions were high. I received positive feedback from my supervising coach and she was always impressed with my work. Then came the oral examination. I have always been terrified of public speaking. All through school, I would never raise my hand or speak in front of the class. I was too afraid of having the wrong answer. And ever since third grade when I forgot my lines on stage during the school play, I have been deathly afraid to speak in front of a crowd. In fact, I'd do anything not to speak in front of others.

For the oral exam, I was required to lead a coaching session with an examiner while another evaluator sat in the room observing me and scoring my performance. And that is exactly what I tried to do: perform. I felt as if I was back on stage as a third grader, and I just froze. I forgot my lines! I felt awful about the session, and I worried for the next three weeks while I waited for my score to arrive in the mail. When I finally received it, I opened the envelope to find a white letter folded in three sections. I practically kept my eyes closed as I slowly unfolded the note. I squinted, then opened my eyes all the way and began reading the first line: "We are sorry to report that you have not met passing requirements for the oral exam." Oh! My heart sank and my stomach knotted into a ball. All the practice, preparation, and studying, and I had not passed! I knew how to be a life coach and a good one at that, but I had tried to "perform" in front of the examiner instead of just being confident in what I had learned. I had become so terrified of the possibility of failure that it came true! All I wanted to do was be a life coach and this seemed like a big door slammed in my face. I was so incredibly disappointed.

At first I felt like this was the universe telling me I was meant to stay stuck in the G.I. lab and that my saboteur had been completely right all along. Maybe I *really wasn't* smart enough to learn these new skills, and I *really wasn't* good enough to make this career change. A few weeks later, after I started to recover from the let down, I tried to focus on what was true. I *could* re-take the test, and I *could* still become a coach. Yes, it was frustrating. I would have to wait for the next round of tests, be nervous again, and pay for the exam again, but I *could* have a second chance. I knew now how badly I wanted to become a life coach. I also realized that I needed to get over my fear of speaking in front of others. And then I realized my dream didn't have an expiration date. I decided I was going to progress forward and I was, in fact, going to become a public speaker.

I applied to take the test again, and this time I made sure I didn't over-prepare or try to put on a show. I just came as myself, stayed present in the moment, and did what I normally would during a real coaching session. I connected to the examiner and didn't allow the words "examination," "test," or "final" to enter into my brain. As soon as it was over, I knew I had done well, and a few weeks later, I received the news that I had passed with flying colors. I earned my certification and gathered more and more clients until I finally quit my nursing job. If I hadn't re-taken the exam and had given into the saboteur, my dreams would still be floating around as just that: dreams. I would still be in that dungeon of a G.I. lab. Thankfully I moved past my disappointment and even my embarrassment, and my dreams are now my reality! As painful as that first oral exam was, it taught me that I *did* want to become a public speaker and facilitator. I wanted to be comfortable in front of people so I would be able to put on retreats and workshops. Now during my workshops I still get a little nervous, but my presentations are second nature.

## Dealing with Disappointment, Step 1: Let it Go!

Sometimes our goals aren't met as soon as we would like them to be or even in the manner in which we thought they would be accomplished. But don't worry! Your dreams don't have expiration dates. There is still time to make them come true. Realize that everyone goes through disappointment. It is how we move past it that counts. It's similar to the feeling of reaching a false peak on a mountain; these little setbacks often come with a lesson, a piece of awareness, or some other wisdom that we can glean about our experience. I've wanted to stop and turn back many times on those tricky false peaks, but I knew that what was on the other side would be so much more rewarding if I figured out how to move past them and keep on reaching for the summit.

What disappointments have you experienced throughout this process? What do you wish you would have done more of or done differently?

_____
_____
_____
_____
_____
_____
_____
_____

What messages did you receive from your saboteur? How have you allowed yourself to be disappointed? That's right: feelings are a choice. You can choose not to stay in your disappointed state.

_____
_____
_____
_____
_____
_____
_____
_____

Instead of believing the saboteur's lies and throwing in the towel, focus on what is REALLY true. What opportunities still exist? What have you learned from your disappointment?

_____
_____
_____
_____
_____
_____
_____

Now, let go of any negative thoughts, messages, or feelings. Do something to release this disappointment, and then start again. Maybe you received a letter of denial, you were turned down after an interview, or you failed a test. What can you do? You could crumple up your score or letter and throw it away. You could reapply for the exam, apply for another position, or send your book to another publisher—but with a renewed confidence in your future acceptance or score. You could also take a hot bath and allow your disappointment to dissolve down the drain. Or you could physically wipe off your shoulders, brushing the disappointment away. You could also recite a positive mantra or post one around your house or office to ward off your saboteur.

I will....

_____

_____

_____

_____

_____

_____

_____

_____

## Dealing with Disappointment, Step 2: If at First You Don't Succeed, Try, Try Again!

We've all had this statement (and others such as "practice makes perfect") drilled into our heads since we were small children. But it is meaningful. Not many successful people were successful on their very first try. Cut yourself some slack and remember we may have to be told "no" over and over again, before we finally receive one "yes." President Barack Obama told students in his back-to-school speech of 2009, *"Some of the most successful people in the world are the ones who've had the most failures. J.K. Rowling's first Harry Potter book was rejected twelve times before it was finally published. Michael Jordan was cut from his high school basketball team, and he lost hundreds of games and missed thousands of shots during his career. But he once said, "I have failed over and over and over again in my life. And that is why I succeed."*

Think of other times you were told "no" or weren't successful on the first try. How many jobs did you get on the first interview? Did you stop looking for a job at all? No, you applied again and again and interviewed over and over until you were finally hired. What do you need to do *again* to move past your disappointment? If you haven't experienced any disappointments in this journey yet, how will you react when you do?

_____

_____

_____

_____

_____

_____

_____

_____

_____

_____

_____

_____

_____

Look up the definition of "determination" in the dictionary or in a thesaurus. Record its meaning and synonyms here. What would it look like for you to practice determination during this last stretch of the journey?

_____
_____
_____
_____
_____
_____
_____
_____

Determination means....

_____
_____
_____
_____
_____
_____
_____

For me, determination looks like...

_____
_____
_____
_____
_____
_____
_____

We all go through disappointment. It is a fact of life. And often when we set out to accomplish our goals, we don't check them off as quickly or as easily as we had planned. This is perfectly normal for us human beings, and you should expect a few bumps in the road along the way. For instance, there is one set of mountains my family and I had set out to climb but, with each attempt, we ran into disappointment. The mountains are in southwest Colorado, three 14ers standing right next to each other: Eolus, Windom, and Sunlight.

In 2007, I purchased tickets for my family and me to ride the Durango and Silverton Narrow Gage Railroad and then backpack into the Chicago Basin area. We had our whole trip scheduled for a weekend in August, and we had been really excited about it. My daughter-in-law had just received her elementary school teaching license that summer and had been hired a few weeks before the term started. The night we were going to drive to Durango ended up being the same night her principal had scheduled a back-to-school open house. As a first year teacher, she couldn't ask for the night off, and we had to put our trip off an entire year.

Luckily, the train station transferred our tickets for a weekend in the summer of 2008. However, a month or so before our trip, my oldest son Greg injured his knee playing hockey. We debated what we should do since I had already spent around one hundred dollars on each train ticket. After much back and forth discussion about safety, timing, and money, we decided to call off the trip once again. We held our tickets as we had done the summer before, hoping that a third time would be the charm.

Over the 4th of July weekend in 2009, we finally made

it out to Durango. Riding a train into the mountains and being dropped off in the middle of nowhere was an amazing experience. We hiked in about 6 miles and set up camp in the middle of a breathtaking basin. The next morning we were off to our usual late start, tired from the long drive down and then the hike in with heavy packs. After climbing a long, steep, grueling trail, we stopped at a lake near the base of the three peaks to eat lunch. Clouds were already making their way overhead. We decided to go for Eolus, the closer of the three, and kept our fingers crossed to ward off bad weather.

About two-thirds of the way up, we ran into a snow field on the steep, steep mountain face. Still the clouds were coming, and they were beginning to darken. We began to brainstorm a strategic way to climb through the snow, but we were worried about the next part of the mountain. We had done our research, and we knew what obstacles were yet to come. At the top of this peak, there was a catwalk, just a few feet across with complete drop-offs on either side. After the catwalk, the summit could be reached by making a class 4 climb (this is rock climbing without gear at around 13,800 feet—crazy!!!) up vertical boulders. We were already nervous about this mountain, and with the threat of melting snow and a potential storm, we just couldn't risk it. Again, we were disappointed as we turned back and retraced our steps down the mountain. We only had one climbing day left, enough for two mountains, but not for three. Eolus would have to wait.

Three summers we spent trying to climb these three mountains, only to return with two checked off the list. It was an expensive, nerve-racking trip, but it was a great one. As I look back, I am grateful our trip was postponed for those two years. By the time we went, my youngest son, Matt, was older, and Greg and Stef were in better shape. We were better prepared for the intense hiking of the Chicago Basin. And yet, we still weren't able to accomplish all of our goals. In fact, just as we returned to our camp after our failed ascent of Eolus, the sun emerged from the clouds, and shone brightly. It was almost as if the mountain itself was basking in our disappointment.

What I learned from that trip is that nothing is ever perfect in life, but that it's also important to savor the things you *have* accomplished and to use those accomplishments to spur you on toward fulfilling other aspirations. Don't ever stop dreaming! Let both your achievements and your disappointments inspire you to keep going.

*"One's best success comes after their greatest disappoint-ments."*

-Eliza Tabor

## One Step Closer...

What have you learned from previous disappointments? How can you use those lessons to help you move closer to your dream? Take any disappointments you've had in pursuing your dream, roll them into a ball, and tuck them away. Look at your goal with new vigor, and write down ways that you're going to regroup and proceed.

_____

_____

_____

_____

_____

_____

_____

_____

_____

_____

_____

_____

_____

_____

_____

_____

_____

_____

_____

_____

_____

_____

False peak at Sunshine Peak
(front) Stef and Greg,
(back) Matt, Kirby, and Deb

CHAPTER TEN

# *Dreams to Reality*
## *Standing on the Summit!*

*"It is not the mountain we
conquer but ourselves"*
- Edmund Hillary

# ⚇ *Chapter Ten* ⚇

At the top of every mountain, you will find a unique and exceptional view. Some summits reach up into a rocky precipice, making for a crowded mass of hikers at the top, while others spread wide and flat, with plenty of room for picnic lunches and group photos. Some peaks are speckled with outstanding reds, oranges, or yellows and others bask in a simple, dull gray.

Regardless of its size, shape, colors, or crevices, each peak possesses an equivalent entity: its view. You are some 14,000 feet high above the rest of the world. You look out and see a vast sea of mountains. Your eyes reach deep down into canyons and valleys through forests of trees. Then they aim up, up, up into the heavens filled with white, wispy strands of clouds which you can almost touch.

You stand there for a few minutes. Your body is weary from the climb: shoulders aching, feet throbbing, sweat dripping. Yes – your body is exhausted, but your spirit is alive, awakened, refreshed! You realize you have not simply conquered this mountain, you have conquered yourself. You have pushed harder, reached further, dug deeper than you ever thought you could. You are standing on top of the world.

And then you look out and realize how many other peaks exist among this one you are standing upon. To the East, to the West, the North and the South, they are endless. Rows and rows of mountain tops are applauding your accomplishment. You stand grounded on this stage of rocks and then bow to your audience, knowing you have performed well, and have gained the respect of the mountains. You breathe deep, taking it all in. You realize other peaks are all you can see.

Dear dreamers, this is what it feels like to be on top of a mountain. To know all the hard work has paid off, to know the obstacles are long behind you, to have persevered past disappointment, pain, or failure. And you are here. You have reached your summit. Take a moment, look around, and drink it all in. Savor this feeling of accomplishment. The view may appear as if it has emerged from a dream world, but it is now your reality. Though you may be weary, exhausted from the journey, I hope your spirit is alive in this place.

Often, when I have summited a peak, I slide my pack off, lay back, sprawled over a rock, and I listen to the stillness. I feel the warmth of the sun kissing my cheeks, and the coolness of the ground on my back, and I recite a prayer thanking God for my safety, asking for protection on the journey back down, and wisdom to receive the lessons from this mountain. And I breathe, in and out, in and out.

## Dreams to Reality,
## Step 1: Stand on the Top!

You are there! You have reached your summit! Stop and be still for a while. Breathe in your success and savor the view from here. What do you see when you look down? Out? Up? Reflect on the feeling of doing what you set out to do. How does it feel?

_____

_____
_____
_____
_____
_____

_____

Go back to Chapter Two. Look at your commitment contract. You signed, dated, and initialed this contract long ago. Maybe you are past the date when you wanted to complete your goal. It doesn't matter. You have adhered to the contract and to your commitment to your dreams. Sometimes I plan to reach a peak around 11am, but if I get there at 1pm, I am never disappointed, as long as I have reached the summit. Stand firm on this peak and celebrate your success. Acknowledge that you have completed your journey and your dreams are now reality.

At the top of many mountains is a registry: a book where you can write your name, adding to the roster of those who have summited the peak. Signing the registry is one of my favorite parts about making it to the top. I always get emotional as I put pen to paper to sign my name and the names of my family members. It's part of the celebration of making all 14,000 feet of the climb. This registry is usually located right next to a marker bolted into the mountain, stamped by the U.S. Geological Survey stating the mountain's exact elevation. Signing this registry not only helps you publicly acknowledge your feat, it also allows you to acknowledge those who came before you and those who will come after you. The registry puts you in the company of other successful strivers.

# Dreams to Reality,
## Step 2: Celebrate

After you sign the certificate of completion on page 186 make a goal of sharing this success with at least three people who haven't already received the good news. This could be a friend or family member, but maybe there is a past mentor or teacher you might contact, someone who will be pleased to hear of your success. Commit to calling them or getting together with them so you can share and fully enjoy your achievements. This doesn't mean bragging, but simply recognizing your determination and hard work and allowing another person to validate it. Who knows? You may even encourage them to take action to reach toward their own dreams. Be proud of yourself, and ask them to celebrate with you.

Honor your achievement through an act of celebration. You get to choose exactly how. Allow me to provide you with a few examples. For instance, when I published this book, I set up a launch party. I invited my closest friends, family members, and many clients to celebrate with me. I was able to thank those who made this project possible, share my experience, and then take pleasure in signing my first printed copies. You might have a book signing or launch party, graduation party, housewarming party, baby shower, or even a small family barbecue depending on the dream you are celebrating. Or you could provide yourself with a personal gift: get a makeover, do a professional photo shoot, take a trip, purchase a new wardrobe, go out on the town with friends, or purchase that piece of furniture you have had your eye on. Whatever you choose, allow yourself to experience joy and gratitude.

# Dreams to Reality,
# Step 3: Descend and Reflect

### One Cannot Stay on the Summit Forever
*One cannot stay on the summit forever;*
*one has to come down again.*
*So why bother in the first place?*
*Just this:*
*What is above knows what is below,*
*but what is below does not know what is above.*
*One climbs, one sees.*
*One descends, one sees no longer, but one has seen.*
*There is an art of conducting oneself in the lower regions*
*by the memory of what one has seen higher up.*
*When one can no longer see, one can at least still know.*
-Rene Daumal

This quote is so true. As a hiker, you never know what you will experience until you have made the climb. Once you are standing on the summit, you can see all that is below you and how incredibly far you have journeyed. As you make your way back down you must retrace your steps, remembering the way you came.

Skim back through the pages of this book, beginning with Chapter One up until Chapter Ten. Revisit your journal entries, the exercises, the experiences you had, and the lessons you learned. Remember the way you came and what it took to get to this place. Reflect on your entire journey.

What are you most proud of?

_____
_____
_____

_____

_____

_____

What would you have done differently?

_____

_____

_____

_____

_____

What did you learn from the obstacles, frustrations, road-blocks, etc.?

_____

_____

_____

_____

_____

What have you learned about yourself as a person? As a dreamer?

_____

_____

_____

_____

_____

What have you seen that you want to remember when you return to the "lower regions?" What do you now know?

_____

_____

_____

_____

_____

Think back on the last six months. Record all the things you have accomplished during this time in a list below.

_____

_____

_____

_____

Are there items on this list you find surprising? Are there some that bring a huge smile to your face? Can you celebrate even the little things? What do you notice most from this list?

_____

_____

_____

_____

_____

## Dreams to Reality,
## Step 4: There is More!

You've reached your goal. You are standing on the summit.

And yet there's more...Can you see the other peaks out there? Do you see the endless possibilities in your future? You would think that at 14,000 feet high you would only see clouds and sky. But in the Rocky Mountains, there are hundreds of peaks. When I am looking out, I am reminded that there are more mountains to conquer, more dreams to think up, and more lessons to learn.

You are not done. Part of celebrating victory is realizing you can do more! Savor the moment, but allow it to inspire you to pursue other dreams you have.

Let me share an example. I had a client who was overweight all her life. She grew up being teased about her body so much she wanted to hide, to become invisible. After we started working together, she totally transformed her eating habits and began working out with a trainer. In one year's time she lost over one hundred pounds! And this is a woman who had never done a day of formal exercise in her life. She had always been too embarrassed about her weight to step into a gym. Once she reached her 100 pound goal, however, she realized that she was capable of a lot more than she ever thought. She started to think about other bridges she wanted to cross — and now she's training for a triathlon!

## Dreams to Reality,
## Step 5: What's Next?

Have you done more than you thought you would? Do you realize now how many mountains are out there? What is next for your future? How can this victory spur you on to your next endeavor?

_____

_____

_____

_____

_____

_____

So here you are. You've filled your pack with equipment, moved long past the trailhead, paced yourself through the trees, followed the trail up steep curves and around jagged boulders, stopped to smell the flowers, climbed over false peaks, and pushed up the last, steep, stretch leading to the summit. Take in the view and see the big picture. Celebrate, reflect, and savor your victories. Climbing this mountain was no small task, was it?

I too remember my first 14er, Mount of the Holy Cross. And when I first stood on that peak, my breath was taken away, lost in the magnificent view. I became hooked. It was then that I truly began to dream. Dear friends, this is just the beginning. Are you dreaming? Dream about the other "mountains" waiting for you. Dream about accomplishing the unthinkable. Dream nonetheless, because, well... dreaming is in your blood.

*"You know you're in love when you can't fall asleep because reality is finally better than your dreams."*

\- Dr. Seuss

## One Step Closer...
Complete your certificate below. Best of luck for your future climbs!

---

### CERTIFICATE OF COMPLETION

*Reach Your Summit and Beyond*
presents this award of achievement to

_____

(name)

On the _____ day of _____
in the year _____.

CONGRATULATIONS!

You have reached the summit of

_____
_____.

(big goal or dream)

Signed

_____

---

Mount Lady Washington with Longs Peak
in the background, Deb and Greg

Top of Notch Mountain with Mount Holy Cross
in the background, Kirby, Matt, and Deb

Uncompahgre Peak,
Kirby and Deb

Red Cloud Peak,
Kirby, Matt, Deb, Stef and Greg

# ≋ *References* ≋

Beattie, Melody. 1992. *Codependant No More: How to Stop Controlling Others and Start Caring for Yourself.* Center City, MN: Hazelden Foundation.

Bridges, William. 1991. *Managing Transitions: Making the Most Out of Change.* New York: Perseus Books.

Brown, Byron. 1998. *Soul Without Shame: A Guide to Liberating Yourself From the Judge Within.* Boston: Shambhala.

Byrne, Rhonda. 2006. *The Secret.,* New York: Atria Books.

Canfield, Jack. 2007. *The Success Principles: How to Get from Where You Are to Where You Want to Be.* New York: HarperCollins.

Capacchione, Lucia. 2000. *Visioning: Ten Steps to Designing the Life of Your Dreams.* New York: Tarcher.

Carson, Rick. 2003. *Taming Your Gremlin: A Surprisingly Simple Method for Getting Out of Your Own Way.* New York: HarperCollins.

Gawain, Shakti. 2002. *Creative Visualization: Use the Power of Your Imagination to Create What You Want in Your Life.* Novato, CA: New World Library.

McGee-Cooper, Ann, et. al. 1992. *You Don't Have To Go Home From Work Exhausted! A Program to Bring Joy, Energy, and Balance to Your Life*. New York: Bantam Books.

Pressfield, Steven. 2002. *The War of Art: Break Through the Blocks and Win Your Inner Creative Battles*. New York: Warner Books.

Price, Catherine. 2009. *Gratitude: A Journal*. California: Chornicle Books.

Whitworth, Laura, et. al. 1998. *Co-Active Coaching: New Skills for Coaching People Toward Success in Work and Life*. Mountain View, CA: Davies-Black Publishing .

# ∿ *About the Author* ∿

Deb Roffe is the founder of Summit Life Coaching. Since 2005, Deb has been coaching clients of all ages and from all walks of life to help them achieve and exceed both professional and personal goals. Also a registered nurse, Deb provides coaching services to professionals in the medical field through The Nurse Coach.

She lives in Denver, Colorado with her husband Kirby. She continues to climb with her three sons, and her daughters-in-law.

You can reach Deb at www.SummitLifeCoaching.net or www.TheNurseCoach.com where you can find more information about her services, workshops, and retreats.

Made in the USA
Charleston, SC
18 April 2011